Made. by Lia

Everyday Craft Baking

Lia Holter

REEDY PRESS

Reedy Press
PO Box 5131
St. Louis, MO, 63139, USA
reedypress.com

Design by Richard Roden

LOC: 2025936462
ISBN: 9781681065519

Printed in Canada
25 26 27 28 29 5 4 3 2 1

Table of Contents

Foreword

I still remember meeting a younger Lia back on August 29, 2014, more than a decade ago now. A mutual friend of ours, Bill Donius, introduced us over breakfast at The Original Pancake House in nearby Ladue, Missouri. Bill, the former chairman and CEO of Pulaski Bank, has always had a certain knack of creating networks and connecting people. Lia was fresh off a major accomplishment of being television's "Next Great Baker." At the same time, AB Mauri North America was preparing to move from nearby Chesterfield into a cool, hip, innovative district just west of downtown St. Louis.

We were both finding our way in new wide-open spaces. Lia had an expanding business that outgrew her home kitchen, while AB Mauri was starting to make its presence known. The circumstances were perfect for collaboration. Lia embodied everything our company needed at the time—youthful energy, the strive for perfection, and a genuine passion for baking. She was a bit of an old soul, too, treasuring family recipes, valuing her local community, and trusting new relationships. Lia was ideal as a newly minted brand ambassador for iconic Fleischmann's Yeast and our collection of brands.

Flash forward several years after Lia's appearances at North America's largest baking show, her annual accolades for top-tier wedding cakes, and a national tour supporting a new PBS television series. It is now easy to see that Lia has come a long way, continuing to evolve her Made. by Lia baking business.

Lia tells her story perfectly and with much grace in the introduction, so I won't attempt to compete with that. Her focus on faith, family, and, frankly, flawless sweet goods really has done the talking for her. I'm no polished baker myself, but as someone who enjoys freshly baked goods made with great intention and purpose, I know you will enjoy taking in *Made. by Lia: Everyday Craft Baking*. Like Lia, the recipes inside are welcoming, new age nostalgic, and utterly incredible. Take in every bite but be sure to share with others. For sure, that's the Lia way.

Rick Oleshak
AB Mauri

Introduction

HOME

The kitchen has always been my home. As a kid—the youngest of five—I found happiness there, surrounded by family. My mom, somehow, always put dinner on the table, even when money was tight. Looking back, my fondest memories revolve around food and loved ones. I'm deeply nostalgic; a single scent or bite can whisk me back to my mom's kitchen, where I grew up as her "sous chef." It's my zen, my happy place. After a long day baking at work, you'll still find me in my kitchen, cooking simple meals with my kids.

My earliest kitchen memory is sitting with my great-grandma Sue, Mema, and Mom, rolling giuggiulena—my favorite Italian cookie. In my family, learning this was an initiation. No measuring cups for sugar or sesame seeds—it's not science, it's heart, tradition, and a whole lotta love. Baking, for me, is an art, a creative outlet. People say it's a scary "science," but I'm here to tell you it doesn't have to be. I'll tweak recipes, adding a pinch of this or that. Sure, precision matters sometimes, but there's room for your personal touch.

At the bakery, I've got every tool and space imaginable to craft small-batch, from-scratch recipes. At home, I keep it simple—I love getting my hands dirty. Kneading dough? I'm in! It's a satisfying, timeless task that takes me back to when life felt uncomplicated. Without a mixer at home, I've rediscovered the basics, like generations before me: a bowl, a workbench, and two hands kneading love into every bite. Using your hands teaches you the craft—feeling when the dough's ready, when a cake springs back, or when a cookie's crackled just right. It takes time and patience, but I'm here to guide you on your baking journey. My recipes are simple, repeatable staples—not one-off showpieces—meant to root themselves in your home, to be shared and passed down.

FAMILY

It takes a village to raise a family and run a business. At the heart of Made. by Lia is family. I am blessed with four incredible kids: three who fill our home with laughter (and chaos!)—Ella, James, and Naomi—and Frances who watches over us from above. My husband, Max, my rock and cheerleader, stands beside me, encouraging me to chase my dreams while we build our own together. Both of our families have been in our corner since the beginning—relentless supporters who've cheered us on every step of the way.

My kids, eager to learn with hands ready to help, are often making messes in the kitchen. Messes that have turned into some of our favorite

recipes at home or at the shop. Sharing the love of cooking with them fuels my creativity and brings me so much joy.

My family is everything to me—the core of who I am. They are the constant reminder of what truly matters at the end of the day. Family will always come first . . . except for when my buttercream is ready, then they'll have to wait. (If you know, you know!)

NEXT GREAT BAKER

In 2014, I competed on *Next Great Baker* with Buddy Valastro, the Cake Boss. I packed a suitcase for an adventure—expecting a week away but ready for two months. Ten teams from across the country tackled over-the-top cakes and wild challenges, with one eliminated each episode. My teammate Al and I (Team Blue) kept pushing forward. It was intense, but it built my confidence and grit. By the finale, I thought, "Dang, we might actually win this!" The prize? $100,000 (split) and a "chance" to run Buddy's new Carlo's Bakery in Las Vegas—a dream at the time.

Faith carried me through. I'd whip out prayer cards and a pocket rosary for courage, despite the producers' puzzled looks. "Why the cards?" they'd ask. "Because I've got God on my side!" I'd reply. For the finale, we had 12 hours to build a cake in the Venetian Hotel. Buddy handed me and the other team keys, saying, "One will open the door to a whole new life." I pulled a prayer card from my "prayer pocket," saw the word "victory," and stepped up. My key worked. Victory! I collapsed in tears (dramatic, I know), and when I looked up, my family and boyfriend (now husband) were there—after two months apart.

Post-win, Vegas tempted me: a 20-something with a shot to work with the Cake Boss in Sin City. But a nudge in my heart said, "Stay home, get married, build roots that dig deep." So, I did.

BUSTING AT THE SEAMS

Winning opened doors fast. My social media blew up, and I was baking commercial quantities from my tiny apartment kitchen—literally busting at the seams. I'd haul cakes down steps, through a parking lot, down a hill, and into my aunt and uncle's basement freezer. Hustle defined me: running a small business, working two jobs, baking into the early hours. I needed space to grow, but where?

A PLACE TO GROW

By 2015, my husband Max and I were hunting for a commercial space in St. Louis. Nothing felt right until a pivotal moment: I met Rick from AB Mauri (Fleischmann's Yeast). He asked me to be their brand ambassador, and my path shifted. I traveled to trade shows, baked thousands of desserts in kitchens across the country, and ran Made. by Lia out of their state-of-the-art baking hub in St. Louis. From my crammed apartment to that dream space, I scaled up, taking 10 times more orders and growing my brand fast.

CHASING MY DREAM

I'd dreamed of owning a bakery since I was a kid. In 2012, I started Made. by Lia as a little Facebook page with big hopes. By 2018, with my daughter Ella at 2, I faced a crossroads: Keep baking from home or open a storefront? It felt daunting. I'd stroll Old Town Flo Town (Florissant) with Ella, peering into a particular storefront, thinking, "That'd make a cute bakery." It wasn't for sale—until it was.

We toured it, but I hesitated, unsure if it was God's plan. I prayed for a sign. Cherry blossoms—symbols of life's fragility and beauty—have marked my journey: both for the *Next Great Baker* finale and tattooed on my wrist. One Sunday, a Blessed Is She email titled "That Terrifying Jump" hit my inbox. It spoke of trusting God's call: "When He calls, He provides." After Mass, I asked Max to drive by the property. There, in the window, sat a faux cherry blossom tree—unseen before, despite countless pass-bys and an empty tour days earlier. In December? A cherry blossom tree? It was my sign. God was saying, "Take the jump—I'll catch you."

BOOM

We opened mid-COVID in 2020, with a 3-year-old, a 1-year-old, and me working 16-hour days—mopping floors at midnight, dreaming of a dishwasher. Despite delays, we launched with a bang, buoyed by community excitement. With lines down the street and a small crew hustling to crank out sweets, we were boomin' and, frankly,

still are. From just me baking and Max washing dishes, Made. by Lia has grown to a team of 20-plus amazing bakers, baristas, and dishwashers.

My team—my bake fam—pours heart and talent into every creation and brings joy to every customer who walks through the door. They've shaped Made. by Lia alongside me, past, present, and future.

COMMUNITY

At Made. by Lia, you'll feel at home—cozy, warm, inviting. It's a place where everyone knows each other, or makes you feel like they do. Old Town Flo Town is where I live, work, and raise my kids—all within blocks. A golf cart ride or 60-second walk gets me from my door to the bakery's back entrance. With baby Naomi now here, I balance business and nursing from my office. Investing in this "small" community—overlooked by some—has been a blessing. Max and I took the leap, unsure where it'd lead but certain this was home.

COOKBOOK

Writing a cookbook overwhelms me with gratitude for the blood, sweat, and tears behind it. This is my calling. I've honed these recipes—many born at home with my kids, developed alongside my team, or passed down from loved ones. They define me as a baker and fuel my bakery's success. Cooking is my love language, connecting me to others through a single bite. When someone says my bakes recall their childhood, that's why I do this: to bring families back to the kitchen, making memories around the table. This book is just the start—I've got so much more to share. Thanks for joining my journey, whether from day one or today. Welcome to my kitchen, my bakery, my home.

Made by Lia
CRAFT BAKERY
BAKERY
CAKES
COFFEE
SWEETS
SWAG

Acknowledgments

Thanks be to God for the courage to live boldly and to share the talents He gave me with others.

This book would not have been possible without the love and support of many who have been by my side throughout my journey. Like I said earlier, it takes a village. My village—family, parents, friends, employees, customers, and fans near and far. Ya'll have helped bring Made. by Lia to life, and I am forever grateful for your constant love, support, and encouragement to keep chasing my dreams.

So many hands have helped bring this book to reality. Special thanks to all who have been involved, at any capacity, whether their hands were covered in flour, lending a hand with watching my kids, or extending their arms for a hug. I appreciate YOU so much.

To my hubby, thanks for taking the jump with me. I love this life we've created together. You're my rock, the best husband and father a gal could ask for, and my best friend. Thank you for having coffee ready in the mornings, for being my forever dishwasher and delivery boy, and for showing me what love is every day.

To my kiddos, you are my inspiration. You remind me every day that the best moments are ones we spend together. There are many ways to say "I love you," but my favorite way is the cooking way.

To my parents, I'll never forget opening my first Kitchen Aid mixer on Christmas morning all those years ago. The sacrifices you made ignited my creativity and ultimately helped shape my path. Thank you for always pushing me, believing in me, and rooting me in faith.

To my rock star team (past, present, and future): Through testing, tasting, and perfecting, your help has been vital in making sure these recipes are tried and true. Your creativity, hard work, and dedication have helped us grow to where we are today. Made. by Lia is made by so much more than just me. It's made by my team. I love each of them like family and am so blessed to have a crew who build each other up, cheer each other on, work their butts off, and love my business like their own.

To my bro-in-law, Dawson, whose photography captured the spirit of creativity, family, and heart of my bakes: Thank you for your vision and talent; I am excited to see our hard work come to life.

To Rick: My time with AB Mauri included some of my most vital moments in my career, ultimately giving me the space to grow Made. by Lia when I needed it most. To now—giving

me this opportunity to share my bakes with others through this book. Huge thanks to you and the AB Mauri team!

To Reedy Press, my publisher: Thank you for taking a chance on me with my first cookbook and for believing in me to make my dream come true. I am excited to embark on this journey with you and hope this will be the first of many.

Catherine, it was so fun having you by my side throughout the creative process. From keeping us on task with a testing schedule to preparing recipes for photos and styling the shoots in my home, your attention to detail and thoroughness have shaped this book.

To Anne from Kitchen Conservatory: Thank you for graciously taking the time to review, test, and proofread these recipes. Your help gave me the ability to focus on my newborn baby and gave me confidence to have my recipes "book ready."

To all of my new followers out there reading my story for the first time, I am excited my recipes have found their way into your home, and I look forward to sharing my love of baking with you!

NOCO
PERK
sauce

Chapter 1

Scones + Biscuits

Back in 2018, before the bakery was built, I made my first scone in my home kitchen with Ella on my hip. I went for a classic lemon-blueberry combo, which can't be beat. While brainstorming what people would want or expect to see at a bakery, I thought a scone would be a lovely way to showcase my favorite flavors of each season. I never dreamed they'd become our signature and fan-favorite item. We pride ourselves on their light, delicate crumb—always moist, never dry. Our customers rave about them and have said they're the best scones they've ever had!

LIA'S TIP: Prepare your biscuit or scone dough; shape and freeze in an airtight container for up to 1 month. Have them on hand to bake at your leisure; when baked from frozen, no need to defrost!

Lemon Blueberry Scones

(gluten-free)

Yield: 8 scones

The lemon blueberry has been our #1 bestseller since the first day we opened our doors. Last year alone, we made nearly 10,000 of these babies. They're a timeless staple you'll want to bake for friends and family time and time again. With bursts of fresh blueberries and a pop of lemon to brighten them up, the best part is they're gluten-free—and you'd never even know it. Don't have gluten-free flour on hand? No stress—swap it for all-purpose flour if gluten is your friend.

INGREDIENTS

¾ cup unsalted butter, cubed + frozen

2 cups gluten-free flour (Bob's Red Mill 1 to 1 is our fav!)

2 Tablespoons granulated sugar

2 Tablespoons packed brown sugar

1 Tablespoon + ¾ teaspoon baking powder

½ teaspoon salt

½ cup heavy cream + a little to brush the tops of the scones

¼ cup + 3 Tablespoons whole milk

¾ teaspoon white vinegar

1 Tablespoon pure vanilla extract

1 Tablespoon pure maple syrup

1 egg

½ cup blueberries, fresh or frozen

¼ cup raw sugar to sprinkle on top

Lemon glaze:

½ cup powdered sugar

3 Tablespoons heavy cream

Zest from 1 lemon

DIRECTIONS

1. Cut butter into 1-inch cubes; freeze for at least 30 minutes.
2. In a mixing bowl fitted with a paddle attachment or using a pastry blender, combine flour, granulated sugar, brown sugar, baking powder, and salt with the cold butter.
3. Mix on low speed until the butter has broken down to the size of peas. You may need to use your hands to break up the larger chunks of butter.
4. In a separate bowl, whisk together heavy cream, milk, vinegar, vanilla extract, maple syrup, and the egg.
5. Add the wet ingredients into the dry ingredients and mix on low until incorporated. If the dough is too wet, add 1–2 Tablespoons of gluten-free flour at a time until the dough comes together (not too sticky).
6. Add in blueberries. Mix on low until combined. Do not overmix or blueberries will start to bleed!
7. Dump dough onto a floured surface, lightly flour your hands, and flatten the dough into a circle, roughly 8 inches round and 1–1 ½ inches thick.
8. Cut like a pie into eight triangles, gently shaping each piece into approximately 3x3x3-inch triangles.
9. Brush the tops with heavy cream and sprinkle with raw sugar.
10. Arrange on a parchment-lined baking sheet, leaving 2–3 inches in between.
11. Set scones in the freezer to chill until firm, at least 30 minutes.
12. Preheat oven to 375 degrees.
13. Remove tray from freezer and place into the oven to bake for 23–25 minutes, rotating halfway through. Bake until lightly golden brown and the tops spring back when touched.
14. While the scones are baking, prepare lemon glaze by whisking together powdered sugar, heavy cream, and lemon zest until smooth.
15. Remove scones from the oven. Using a piping bag or spoon, drizzle with the lemon glaze.
16. Scones are best served the same day but can be stored in an airtight container for up to 3 days or frozen prior to baking for up to 1 month.

Strawberry Shortcake Scones

Yield: 8 scones

These have become a fan favorite at the shop—craved all year-round but truly the best when strawberries are in season. The scone itself is simple and light, providing the perfect backdrop to let lush strawberries shine. Spoon strawberry glaze over the top while still warm for the dreamiest drip.

INGREDIENTS

½ heaping cup fresh strawberries, sliced + frozen

¾ cup unsalted butter, cubed + frozen

2 cups all-purpose flour

2 Tablespoons granulated sugar

2 Tablespoons packed brown sugar

1 Tablespoon baking powder

½ teaspoon salt

½ cup heavy cream + a little to brush the tops of the scones

¼ cup + 1 Tablespoon whole milk

1 ½ teaspoons pure vanilla extract

1 egg

¾ teaspoon white vinegar

¼ cup raw sugar to sprinkle on top

Strawberry glaze:

1 cup powdered sugar

2 Tablespoons strawberry preserves

¼ cup + 1 Tablespoon heavy cream

DIRECTIONS

1. Slice the strawberries into thin slices and arrange on a parchment-lined sheet tray, and place into the freezer for at least 30 minutes. Or, you can easily buy presliced frozen strawberries in a pinch!
2. Cut butter into 1-inch cubes; freeze for at least 30 minutes.
3. In a mixing bowl fitted with a paddle attachment or using a pastry blender, combine flour, granulated sugar, brown sugar, baking powder, and salt with the cold butter.
4. Mix on low speed until the butter has broken down to the size of peas. You may need to use your hands to break up the larger chunks of butter.
5. In a separate bowl, whisk together heavy cream, milk, vinegar, vanilla extract, and egg.
6. Add the wet ingredients into the dry ingredients and mix on low until incorporated. If the dough is too wet, add 1–2 Tablespoons of flour one at a time until the dough comes together (not too sticky).
7. Add in strawberries. Mix on low until just combined.
8. Dump dough onto a floured surface, lightly flour your hands, and flatten the dough into a circle, roughly 8 inches round and 1–1 ½ inches thick.
9. Cut like a pie into eight triangles, gently shaping each piece into approximately 3x3x3-inch triangles.
10. Arrange on a parchment-lined baking sheet, leaving 2–3 inches in between.
11. Set scones in freezer to chill until firm, at least 30 minutes.
12. Preheat oven to 375 degrees.
13. Remove tray from freezer and place into the oven to bake for 22–25 minutes, rotating halfway through. Bake until lightly golden brown and the tops spring back when touched.
14. While scones are baking, prepare your strawberry glaze. Whisk together powdered sugar, heavy cream, and strawberry preserves until smooth.
15. Remove scones from oven and spoon the strawberry glaze over the scones.
16. Scones are best served the same day but can be stored in an airtight container for up to 3 days or frozen prior to baking for up to 1 month.

Birthday Cake Scones

Yield: 8 scones

These are so fun to make with kids—anything with sprinkles gets them excited about being in the kitchen. I always catch them sneaking a few jimmies whenever they can.

LIA'S TIP: Make and shape the dough the day before so they're ready to pop in the oven for a little birthday breakfast treat. You'll be a hero and start their birthday off right!

INGREDIENTS

¾ cup unsalted butter, cubed + frozen

2 cups all-purpose flour

2 Tablespoons granulated sugar

2 Tablespoons packed brown sugar

1 Tablespoon baking powder

½ teaspoon salt

½ cup heavy cream + more for brushing the tops

¼ cup + 1 Tablespoon whole milk

¾ teaspoon white vinegar

1 ½ teaspoons pure vanilla extract

1 ½ teaspoons almond extract

1 egg

½ cup sprinkles (jimmies), plus more for sprinkling on top

Vanilla glaze:

½ cup powdered sugar

3 Tablespoons heavy cream

¼ teaspoon almond extract

½ teaspoon pure vanilla extract

DIRECTIONS

1. Cut butter into 1-inch cubes; let freeze for at least 30 minutes.
2. In a mixing bowl fitted with a paddle attachment or using a pastry blender, combine flour, granulated sugar, brown sugar, baking powder, and salt with the cold butter.
3. Mix on low speed until the butter has broken down to the size of peas. You may need to use your hands to break up the larger chunks of butter.
4. In a separate bowl, whisk together heavy cream, milk, vinegar, vanilla extract, almond extract, and egg.
5. Add the wet ingredients into the dry ingredients and mix on low until incorporated. If the dough is too wet, add 1–2 Tablespoons of flour one at a time until the dough comes together (not too sticky).
6. Add in jimmies. Mix on low until just combined.
7. Dump dough onto a floured surface. Shape into an 8-inch circle 1–1 ½ inches thick.
8. Using a round biscuit cutter, cut dough into circles; use scraps and shape into a circle. Or, alternatively, cut the dough like a pie into eight triangles, and gently shape each into approximately 3x3x3-inch triangles.
9. Brush the tops with heavy cream and sprinkle with raw sugar.
10. Arrange on a parchment-lined baking sheet, leaving space between, and chill in the freezer until firm at least 30 minutes.
11. Preheat oven to 375 degrees.
12. Remove tray from freezer and place into the oven to bake for 22–25 minutes, rotating halfway through. Bake until lightly golden brown and the tops spring back when touched.
13. While scones are baking, prepare the vanilla glaze by whisking together powdered sugar, heavy cream, almond extract, and vanilla extract until smooth.
14. Remove scones from oven, spoon the glaze over the scones, and sprinkle with jimmies.
15. Scones are best served the same day but can be stored in an airtight container for up to 3 days or frozen prior to baking for up to 1 month.

Cheddar Chive Scones

Yield: 8 scones

Every bakery needs a savory option to balance all the sweetness. I, for one, am always craving something salty after being surrounded by sweets all day. Once we saw how popular our blueberry scone was, we knew we needed a savory scone on the menu, and a classic cheddar chive was just the ticket. It's basically a glorified version of the Red Lobster biscuit—buttery and tender, perfect on its own, especially served warm right out of the oven.

INGREDIENTS

¾ cup cold unsalted butter, cubed + frozen

2 cups all-purpose flour + extra if needed

1 Tablespoon baking powder

¾ teaspoon granulated sugar

¾ teaspoon salt

½ cup shredded cheddar

1 Tablespoon chopped parsley

1 Tablespoon chopped chives

½ cup heavy cream

¾ cup + 2 Tablespoons whole milk

¾ teaspoon white vinegar

1 egg

2 Tablespoons heavy cream for brushing the tops

DIRECTIONS

1. Cube butter into 1-inch cubes; freeze for at least 30 minutes.
2. In a mixer fitted with the paddle attachment or by hand using a pastry blender, mix flour, baking powder, sugar, and salt with the cubed frozen butter.
3. Mix on low speed until butter has broken down to the size of peas. You may have to break down the butter more with your hands if needed.
4. Add cheddar and herbs. Mix until incorporated.
5. In a measuring cup, combine cream, milk, vinegar, and egg, and stir.
6. Add the wet ingredients into the dry ingredients. Mix to combine. If the dough is wet and sticky, add 2–4 Tablespoons flour as needed.
7. Remove dough from the bowl and place onto a floured surface.
8. Roll dough into a log shape and using your hands, flatten into a rectangle about 1 ½ inches thick.
9. Cut into eight rectangles and place onto a parchment-lined baking sheet, leaving space in between. Brush the tops with heavy cream.
10. Place into the freezer for at least 30 minutes prior to baking.
11. Preheat oven to 375 degrees.
12. Sprinkle the tops with a little salt and bake for 22–25 minutes until tops are lightly golden brown and spring back when touched.
13. Best served right out of oven but can be stored in an airtight container for up to 3 days or frozen prior to baking for up to 1 month.

Butter Biscuits

Yield: 8 biscuits

My lead baker for several years and dear friend, Kaylene, was gracious enough to share her biscuit recipe with us. They are so simple and whip up in about 10 minutes by hand! Layers upon layers of buttery, flaky goodness. Try them with a smear of homemade jam, drizzle with hot honey, or top with gravy or a fried egg. So dang good!

LIA'S TIP: Have an egg allergy? Use heavy cream instead of egg wash and you'll still get a nice golden color!

INGREDIENTS

1 ½ cups whole milk

1 ½ Tablespoons fresh-squeezed lemon juice

4 cups all-purpose flour + more for sprinkling

2 Tablespoons granulated sugar

2 Tablespoons baking powder

2 teaspoons salt

1 cup unsalted butter, cubed + cold

Egg wash:

1 egg

1 ½ Tablespoons heavy cream or whole milk

HONEY BUTTER SPREAD

½ cup unsalted butter, softened

1 Tablespoon honey

In a small bowl, combine butter and honey; mix together with a spatula until smooth.

HOT HONEY

1 cup local honey

½ Tablespoon chili pepper flakes

Heat honey and chili flakes in a small saucepan until a simmer, remove from heat, and let honey infuse for 15 minutes.

Strain through a fine-mesh sieve and store in an airtight container or jar.

DIRECTIONS

1. In a measuring cup, combine milk and lemon juice to make buttermilk. Let sit for at least 5 minutes.
2. In a mixer fitted with the paddle attachment or by hand (my personal preference!), combine flour, sugar, baking powder, and salt with the cubed butter.
3. On low speed or with your hands, break down the butter to pea size or slightly larger. It's okay if there are some bigger pieces.
4. Add the buttermilk mixture into the dry ingredients. Using a wooden spoon or mixer, stir gently until just combined but not fully incorporated. Don't overmix! The dough may be a bit messy, but don't fret.
5. Dump the dough onto a lightly floured surface, flatten/press into an 8 x 6 rectangle about 1 ½ inches thick.
6. Sprinkle a little flour on top. Using a bench scraper, grab the underside of the dough and fold it in half upward. Rotate the dough 90 degrees and press back into an 8 x 6 rectangle. Sprinkle a little flour between each fold.
7. Repeat this folding process three times for a total of four folds (see diagram).
8. After the last fold, press back into an 8 x 6 rectangle. Using a bench scraper, cut down the center and then cut four across, creating eight rectangles or shape/size of choice.
9. In a separate small bowl, whisk together the egg and 1 ½ Tablespoons heavy cream. Brush the tops with egg wash and arrange on a parchment-lined baking sheet, leaving space in between each biscuit. Or, alternatively, omit the egg and brush the tops with heavy cream.
10. Freeze for at least 30 minutes prior to baking, or freeze for up to 1 month and bake without defrosting (same bake time as directed).
11. Preheat oven to 375 degrees.
12. Bake for 22–25 minutes, rotating the tray halfway through until biscuits have puffed up and have a beautiful golden color on top and bottom.
13. Best served right out of the oven but can be stored in an airtight container for up to 3 days. Toast or warm prior to serving.
14. Top with hot honey, honey butter, or homemade jam.

FOLDING GUIDE

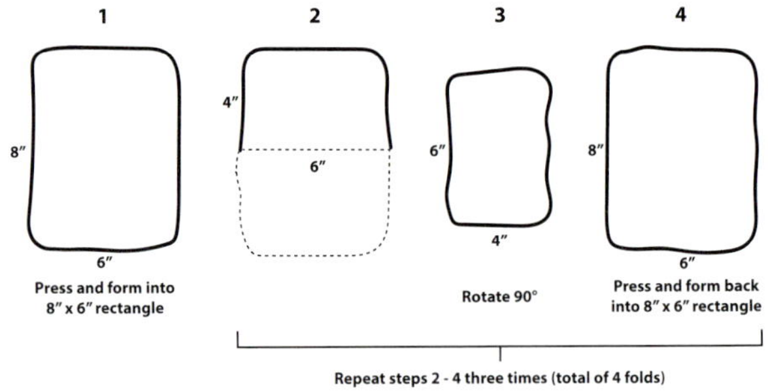

Dill + Goat Cheese Biscuits

Yield: 8 biscuits

Dill is by far my favorite fresh herb. At the bakery, we always have an abundance growing in our little garden right outside the kitchen doors. The fresh dill paired with the tartness of goat cheese creates such a light, fresh flavor, and the smell of summer wafts through the kitchen.

ADDITIONAL INGREDIENTS

2 Tablespoons fresh dill, chopped

3 ounces goat cheese

DIRECTIONS

1. Follow steps for Butter Biscuit dough. Add fresh dill at step 2 with the dry ingredients.
2. Fold 1 ounce of crumbled goat cheese on half of the dough at each fold (see step 7).
3. At step 8 you can either cut the dill biscuits into eight rectangles or use a biscuit cutter to pop out eight round biscuits.
4. Follow the same baking/ storing instructions as directed in the Butter Biscuit recipe.

Chapter 2

Muffins + Quick Breads

Everyone should have a go-to muffin or quick bread recipe ready to whip up for a fast breakfast or snack. There are so many fun flavors to play with, and I love getting my kids in the kitchen to line the tray with cupcake liners, stir, and scoop the batter. These are meant to be simple, no-fuss recipes you can make in a pinch—whether you need a break from laundry or work or want to spread some joy to a neighbor or friend.

Ella Muffins

(vegan + gluten-free)

Yield: 12 muffins or 2 dozen mini muffins

When Ella was about a year old, I created the "Ella Muffin." Bright green and packed with protein from spinach with sweetness from bananas. Ella is my sidekick in the kitchen, and some of my favorite memories include her tiny hands ready to help. These are a great way to sneak in healthy stuff without your kids even noticing. My kids love them! Make them mini to fit in lunches for the perfect-sized treat for your littles.

LIA'S TIP: Don't throw away those overripe bananas! Peel them, place into an airtight bag, and store in the freezer. Perfect for these muffins, banana bread, or smoothies!

INGREDIENTS

2 heaping cups of fresh spinach

½ cup unsweetened almond or dairy-free milk

2 medium ripe bananas, approximately 1 cup, mashed

2 Tablespoons coconut oil, melted

1 cup almond flour

¾ cup all-purpose flour (to make gluten-free, replace all-purpose flour with 1 cup of ground oats)

¼ cup flax meal

2 teaspoons baking powder

½ teaspoon baking soda

½ teaspoon salt

1 teaspoon cinnamon

3 teaspoons raw sugar + more for sprinkling

½–¾ cup wild blueberries, fresh or frozen

DIRECTIONS

1. Preheat oven to 350 degrees and line your muffin pan with liners.
2. In a food processor, puree the spinach and dairy-free milk.
3. Add bananas and oil into the food processor. Blend until smooth. Set aside.
4. In a mixing bowl, whisk together almond flour, flour, flax, baking powder, baking soda, salt, cinnamon, and raw sugar.
5. Pour the spinach mixture into the dry ingredients, and using a spatula, mix together until a smooth batter forms and there are no lumps.
6. Fold in blueberries. (I like wild blueberries since they are mini, but you can totally use regular.)
7. Use an ice cream scoop or spoon to divide the batter evenly among the muffin tins, about ¾ full, and sprinkle tops with raw sugar.
8. Bake at 350 degrees for approximately 20–25 minutes, rotating the tray halfway through, until tops are golden and spring back when touched.
9. Wait until they are completely cooled before you dig in, so the texture has time to develop.
10. Store in an airtight container for up to 2 days or in the freezer for up to 1 month. These are great to have on hand to pop out whenever you need a quick snack!

James's Famous Blueberry Muffins

Yield: 12 muffins

Jamesy used to get jealous when we'd say "Ella Muffins," so he'd call them "me muffins!" That's when I decided he needed his own claim to fame. I'll never forget pulling up a chair to my workbench for him to stand on and asking what he wanted to bake. In his little raspy voice, he said, "Blueberries!"—which wasn't surprising since he ate them by the handful daily. Thus, James's Famous Blueberry Muffins were born. This is the perfect base muffin recipe, versatile enough to use blueberries, any fruit, or even mini chocolate chips.

INGREDIENTS

½ cup unsalted butter, softened

¾ cup granulated sugar

¼ cup packed brown sugar

½ Tablespoon orange or lemon zest (optional)

2 eggs, at room temperature

1 teaspoon pure vanilla extract

2 ¼ cups all-purpose flour

¾ teaspoon salt

2 teaspoons baking powder

½ cup whole milk, at room temperature

¼ cup sour cream or plain yogurt

2 cups fresh blueberries (You can use frozen, but they will turn the batter purple. Still yummy though!)

¼ cup raw sugar for sprinkling

DIRECTIONS

1. Preheat oven to 350 degrees.
2. In a mixing bowl fitted with the paddle attachment or using a wooden spoon, mix together the butter, zest, sugar, and brown sugar until light and fluffy.
3. In a separate bowl, whisk together dry ingredients: flour, salt, and baking powder.
4. Crack eggs into a small measuring cup or bowl and add in vanilla extract. Add the eggs into the butter mixture one at a time, scraping down the bowl after each addition.
5. Add half of the dry ingredients into the mixing bowl. Mix well.
6. Add in the milk and sour cream. Mix to combine. Scape down the sides of the bowl.
7. Add in the rest of the dry ingredients until a smooth batter forms. It will be a little thick, but that's okay!
8. Using a spatula, fold in the fresh blueberries. Do not overmix!
9. Using a cookie scoop or spoon, divide the batter evenly among the muffin tins, approximately ¾ full.
10. Sprinkle the tops with raw sugar and bake for 20–25 minutes, rotating the tray halfway through, until the muffins are lightly golden on top and the cake springs back when you touch it.
11. Let cool before serving.
12. Store in an airtight container for up to 3 days or freeze for up to 1 month.

Pumpkin Spice Muffins

Yield: 1 dozen

Why did society decide pumpkin spice is only for the fall? I look forward to this muffin every year. The smell alone makes you want to slip on your favorite jeans and a hoodie, sit outside, and cozy up with a PSL and this "perfectly spiced muffin."

INGREDIENTS

Muffin batter:

1 ¼ cups all-purpose flour

½ teaspoon salt

1 teaspoon baking powder

1 teaspoon baking soda

½ teaspoon cinnamon

½ teaspoon pumpkin spice

¼ teaspoon ground nutmeg

⅛ teaspoon allspice

½ cup granulated sugar

½ cup packed brown sugar

1 teaspoon pure vanilla extract

¾ cup prepared pumpkin puree

½ cup canola or vegetable oil

2 eggs

2 Tablespoons sour cream

Topping:

¼ cup all-purpose flour

⅛ cup oats

⅛ cup pepitas

3 Tablespoons packed brown sugar

⅛ teaspoon salt

¼ teaspoon cinnamon

¼ teaspoon pumpkin spice

2 Tablespoons unsalted butter, melted

DIRECTIONS

1. Preheat oven to 350 degrees and line a muffin pan with liners.
2. In a bowl, sift together the dry ingredients: flour, salt, baking powder, baking soda, and spices.
3. In a separate mixing bowl fitted with the paddle attachment or by hand with a whisk, mix together granulated sugar, brown sugar, vanilla extract, pumpkin puree, and oil.
4. Add in eggs. Mix to combine.
5. Add in the sour cream and mix until smooth.
6. Slowly add the dry ingredients into the wet ingredients. Scrape down the bowl and mix well to combine.
7. Use a cookie scoop or spoon to divide the batter among the tins, approximately ¾ full.

Topping:

1. In a small bowl, combine flour, oats, pepitas, brown sugar, salt, and spices.
2. Melt butter and pour over the topping ingredients. Mix together by hand or with a fork until a crumble forms.
3. Sprinkle the topping over the muffins and bake for 20–25 minutes, until golden and the top springs back when touched.
4. Let cool before serving, if you can wait that long!
5. Store in an airtight container for up to 3 days or in the freezer for up to 1 month.

Zucchini Bread

Yield: 1 loaf pan

My mom's best friend, Linda, would bring us a loaf of her zucchini bread around Christmastime every year. I remember peeling back the foil, smelling the warm spices, and seeing the perfect crusty layer of powdered sugar dusted on top. Lucky for me (and now you), she shared her secret ingredient, which gives it that nostalgic flavor! I've had many say this recipe reminds them of their grandma's, which is a baker's highest compliment.

INGREDIENTS

1 ½ cups all-purpose flour

½ teaspoon baking powder

½ teaspoon baking soda

½ teaspoon salt

2 teaspoons cinnamon

½ teaspoon pumpkin spice (secret ingredient, shhh!)

1 ½ cups grated zucchini

½ cup granulated sugar

½ cup packed brown sugar

½ cup canola or vegetable oil

2 teaspoons pure vanilla extract

1 egg

Powdered sugar for dusting

DIRECTIONS

1. Preheat oven to 350 degrees.
2. In a mixing bowl, sift together the dry ingredients: flour, baking powder, baking soda, salt, and spices.
3. In a separate bowl, whisk together zucchini, sugar, brown sugar, oil, vanilla extract, and egg.
4. Add the dry ingredients into the wet ingredients and fold gently, making sure there are no lumps, until all ingredients are incorporated well.
5. Spray a loaf pan with cooking spray and pour the batter into the pan.
6. Bake for approximately 1 hour, rotating the pan halfway through.
7. The top should be golden brown, slightly cracked, and spring back when touched.
8. Dust the top with powdered sugar and allow to cool prior to serving.
9. Store wrapped tightly in foil, in an airtight bag or container for up to 3 days, or freeze loaf for up to 1 month.

Cinnamon Swirl Bundt Cake

Yield: 1 bundt cake

Nothing pairs better with a cup of coffee than a slice of this warm, cinnamony, ooey-gooey but not too sweet bundt cake. Bundt cakes are classic—a beautiful centerpiece for brunch or Sunday morning with your family. And don't worry if it doesn't pop out of the pan perfectly; that little crumb makes the perfect baker's snack.

INGREDIENTS

2 ½ cups all-purpose flour

¾ teaspoon baking powder

1 ½ teaspoons sea salt

½ cup shortening

1 cup unsalted butter, softened

2 ½ cups granulated sugar

2 teaspoons pure vanilla extract

5 eggs, at room temperature

1 cup whole milk, room temperature

Cinnamon swirl:

¾ cup packed brown sugar

2 teaspoons cinnamon

1 teaspoon ginger

½ teaspoon allspice

Powdered sugar for dusting

DIRECTIONS

1. Preheat oven to 350 degrees. Spray and lightly flour a 10–12-cup bundt cake pan. (You can use baking spray with flour already in it, which works great!)
2. Sift together the dry ingredients: flour, baking powder, and salt. Set aside.
3. In a mixing bowl fitted with the paddle attachment or using a hand mixer, mix together shortening and softened butter until smooth.
4. Add sugar and mix together until light and fluffy.
5. In a separate bowl, combine vanilla extract with the eggs, and add the eggs into the butter mixture one at a time, scraping down the bowl after each addition.
6. Add in half of the dry ingredients. Gently mix to combine.
7. Add in the milk. Mix to combine.
8. Add in the rest of the dry ingredients. Scrape down the bowl and mix until a smooth batter is formed.

Swirl + assembly:

1. In a small bowl, add brown sugar, cinnamon, ginger, and allspice; stir together. Add in 2 ½ cups of the batter. Stir to combine.
2. Spoon half of the plain batter into the bottom of the prepared bundt pan. Using a spatula, smooth the batter into an even layer.
3. Next, spoon the cinnamon swirl batter on top and spread it into an even layer across the batter.
4. Top with the remaining plain batter and smooth across the top.
5. Place into the oven and bake for approximately 1 hour until the top is golden brown and springs back when touched.
6. Let cool for 20–30 minutes before removing the cake from the bundt pan. You want the pan to be still warm but not hot.
7. Run a small spatula around the edges and place a sheet tray lined with parchment paper or a serving dish on top of the pan. While holding the bottom of the bundt, flip the tray over to invert the pan. Tap the top of the pan to help loosen the cake and carefully release it from the pan.
8. Dust the top with powdered sugar and serve immediately. Wrap tightly and store for up to 3 days or freeze for up to 1 month.

Chapter 3

Donuts vs Doughnuts

A controversial question: What's the difference between a donut and a doughnut? For me, donuts are baked cake donuts, and doughnuts are fried and yeast-raised. Both are delicious in their own way. My baked donuts are actually all allergy friendly—I love creating recipes that surprise people when they take a bite!

Cinnamon Suga' Donuts

(vegan)

Yield: 6 donuts, donut pan required

This is probably one of the recipes I'm proudest of. It was an "aha!" moment after taking the first bite. This donut raises the bar. It's vegan, and you'd honestly never know.

INGREDIENTS

1 flax "egg" (1 Tablespoon ground flax + 2 Tablespoons water)

¼ cup packed brown sugar

¼ cup maple syrup

1 teaspoon vinegar

1 Tablespoon canola oil

1 cup + 1 Tablespoon all-purpose flour

½ teaspoon baking powder

¼ teaspoon baking soda

1 teaspoon cinnamon

½ teaspoon salt

½ cup + 1 Tablespoon canned coconut milk

2 teaspoons pure vanilla extract

For dipping:

2 ounces vegan butter, melted (our fav is Earth Balance)

½ Tablespoon cinnamon

½ cup granulated sugar

DIRECTIONS

1. Preheat the oven to 350 degrees.
2. Spray a donut pan with cooking spray.
3. In a small bowl, combine flax meal and water to create the flax "egg;" let set to thicken.
4. In a separate bowl, sift together flour, baking powder, baking soda, cinnamon, and salt.
5. In a medium mixing bowl, mix brown sugar, maple syrup, vinegar, and oil to combine.
6. Stir in flax egg.
7. Add half of the dry ingredients to the sugar mixture and gently combine.
8. Add in coconut milk and vanilla extract. Mix to combine.
9. Add in the rest of the dry ingredients. Mix until a smooth batter forms.
10. Spoon the batter into a large piping bag, or using a spoon, divide the batter among the prepared donut pans.
11. Bake 12–15 minutes, rotating halfway through, until puffed up, lightly golden, and the top springs back when touched.
12. Let donuts cool slightly, then flip the pan over a lined sheet tray and tap to pop them out of the pan.
13. Dip right away or store in an airtight container and freeze for up to 1 month prior to dipping.

To dip:

1. Melt vegan butter in a bowl big enough for the donut to fit in.
2. In a separate small bowl mix together cinnamon and sugar.
3. Lightly dip the tops and bottoms of the donuts into the vegan butter, scraping off the excess on the side of the bowl.
4. Dunk the donut into the cinnamon sugar, coating the tops, bottoms, and sides. Shake off any extra for an even dusting.
5. Serve immediately, store in an airtight container for up to 3 days, or freeze for up to 1 month.

Lemon Poppy Donuts

(vegan)

Yield: 6 donuts, donut pan required

This recipe started at home during my vegan phase. I was creating a repertoire of vegan dinners but also wanted a treat to indulge in. With a bright, natural lemony color and a pop of fresh lemon flavor, these donuts are oh-so-delicious and even prettier to look at. Topped with a silky glaze and edible flowers, they'll steal the show at any brunch.

INGREDIENTS

Donut batter:

1 flax "egg" (1 Tablespoon ground flax + 2 Tablespoons water)

¼ cup coconut oil, melted

2 Tablespoons vegan butter, melted

¼ cup packed brown sugar

¼ cup granulated sugar

1 ½ teaspoons pure vanilla extract

2 Tablespoons lemon zest (2 lemons)

¾ cup unsweetened almond, coconut, or soy milk

1 Tablespoon fresh lemon juice

1 ¼ cups all-purpose flour

½ teaspoon baking soda

1 teaspoon baking powder

½ teaspoon salt

1 ½ teaspoons poppy seeds

Glaze:

1 cup powdered sugar

1 Tablespoon dairy-free milk

2 Tablespoons fresh lemon juice

Garnish:

1 Tablespoon poppy seeds

Edible flowers (pansies, nasturtium, marigolds, etc.)

DIRECTIONS

1. Preheat oven to 400 degrees. Spray the donut pan with pan spray.
2. In a small bowl, combine ground flax and water to create the flax "egg;" set aside for 5 minutes.
3. In a separate bowl, whisk together the dry ingredients: flour, baking soda, baking powder, and salt.
4. In a mixing bowl fitted with the paddle attachment or using a hand mixer, combine melted coconut oil, vegan butter, brown sugar, granulated sugar, vanilla, and lemon zest. Mix until smooth.
5. Add in flax "egg;" mix to combine.
6. Add in dairy-free milk and lemon juice. Mix to combine.
7. Slowly add the dry ingredients into the wet ingredients, then add in the poppy seeds and mix until smooth.
8. Using a piping bag or spoon, divide the batter among the prepared donut pans, slightly under the rim.
9. Place into the oven and bake for approximately 20 minutes, rotating the tray halfway through, until donuts are lightly golden on top and they spring back when touched.
10. Remove from the oven and let set for 5 minutes before turning the pan over onto a parchment-lined sheet tray, popping out the donuts.
11. Let the donuts cool completely before dipping them into the glaze. You can bake these ahead of time and store in an airtight container in the freezer for up to 1 month prior to dipping.

To dip:

1. Place powdered sugar, dairy-free milk, and lemon juice into a small bowl (big enough for the donut to fit into) and whisk until smooth. Add a splash more dairy-free milk if the mixture is too thick or more powdered sugar if it is too thin. It should look glossy and be of dipping consistency, but not so thin that it absorbs into the donut.
2. Dip your donuts into the glaze and place onto a parchment-lined tray or serving tray.
3. Once all of the donuts have been dipped, sprinkle the tops with poppy seeds and garnish with edible flowers (pansies are my favorite).
4. Store the donuts in the fridge in an airtight container for up to 2 days or freeze without the flowers for up to 1 month.

Chocolate Espresso Donuts

(vegan + gluten-free)

Yield: 6 donuts, donut pan required

This is one sexy, decadent donut. Rich chocolatey flavor enhanced by espresso—one bite feels indulgent, but there's no need for guilt here. These beauties are vegan and gluten-free, and no one will ever know it.

LIA'S TIP: It's super important when it comes to vegan and/or gluten-free items to not overmix the batter. This can affect the bake and cause a gummy texture.

INGREDIENTS

Donut batter:

1 flax "egg" (1 Tablespoon ground flax + 2 Tablespoons water)

1 cup gluten-free flour (my favorite is Bob's Red Mill 1 to 1)

¼ cup + 2 Tablespoons unsweetened cocoa powder

½ teaspoon baking powder

¼ teaspoon baking soda

¼ teaspoon salt

3 Tablespoons canola oil

¼ cup granulated sugar

¼ cup packed brown sugar

1 teaspoon pure vanilla extract

½ cup unsweetened almond milk

3 Tablespoons coconut milk

2 Tablespoons espresso (or instant espresso)

Chocolate glaze:

1 cup vegan chocolate chips

¼ cup almond or dairy-free milk

Espresso glaze:

1 cup powdered sugar

1 Tablespoon vegan butter

1 Tablespoon espresso (or instant espresso)

DIRECTIONS

1. Preheat oven to 350 degrees.
2. In a small bowl, combine the ground flax and water to create the flax "egg." Set aside for 5 minutes.
3. In a separate bowl, sift together the dry ingredients: gluten-free flour, cocoa, baking powder, baking soda, and salt.
4. In a mixing bowl fitted with the paddle attachment or by hand with a whisk, mix together the oil, sugar, brown sugar, and vanilla extract until smooth.
5. Add in the flax "egg" and mix to combine.
6. Add in half of the dry ingredients. Mix to combine.
7. Next add in the almond milk, coconut milk, and espresso; mix to combine.
8. Add in the remaining dry ingredients and mix until they are incorporated; do not overmix. The batter may be a tad lumpy, but that's okay!
9. Spoon the batter into a large piping bag, or using a spoon, divide batter among the prepared donut pan, right to the rim.
10. Bake for 12–15 minutes, rotating the tray halfway through, until the donuts puff up and spring back when touched on top.
11. Remove from the oven and let cool for 5 minutes before inverting the tray and popping the donuts out of the pan onto a parchment-lined sheet tray.
12. Set the donuts aside to cool fully prior to dipping while you prepare the glazes.

Chocolate glaze:

1. In a microwave-safe bowl, combine the vegan chocolate chips and almond milk.
2. Melt in 30-second intervals, stirring after each time.
3. Once the chocolate chips have melted, whisk until silky and smooth. If the glaze seems too thick, add in a splash more almond milk to make it a dippable consistency.

Espresso glaze:

1. In a small bowl, combine powdered sugar, melted vegan butter, and espresso. Whisk until smooth.

Assembly:

1. Dip each donut into the chocolate glaze and set on a parchment-lined tray or serving dish.
2. Fill a piping bag with the espresso glaze, cut a small hole at the end, and drizzle the glaze over each donut. No piping bag? Just use a spoon to drizzle the glaze over the top.
3. Enjoy immediately or store in an airtight container in the fridge for up to 3 days. Can be frozen up to 1 month prior to dipping.

Doughnuts and Dots

Yield: 15 2 ½-inch doughnuts + dots

Now onto a classic, traditional yeast-raised, fried doughnut. Light, fluffy, and not too sweet. When I collaborated with Fleischmann's Yeast, I knew I needed a recipe where yeast was the star. These will become your new weekend routine—prep the dough a day ahead to enjoy the next morning. It's a great way to get kids in the kitchen; let them make the dough, cut out the doughnuts, or dip them in glaze. The dots are my favorite part—little bursts of heaven!

INGREDIENTS

1 cup warm whole milk, 110 degrees

1 packet Fleischmann's Active Dry Yeast (2 ¼ teaspoons)

¼ cup granulated sugar + 1 Tablespoon, divided

¼ teaspoon cinnamon

¼ teaspoon nutmeg

¾ teaspoon salt

4 cups all-purpose flour

2 eggs

6 Tablespoons unsalted butter, melted

1 teaspoon pure vanilla extract

1 ½ cups canola or vegetable oil for frying

Sprinkles for topping (optional)

¼–½ cup powdered sugar for rolling dots

Vanilla glaze:

1 cup powdered sugar

¼ cup + 1 Tablespoon heavy cream

½ teaspoon pure vanilla extract

DIRECTIONS

1. Whisk together warm milk, yeast, and 1 Tablespoon sugar. Let sit 5 minutes.
2. In a separate bowl, add in the flour, ¼ cup sugar, and spices. Make a well and add the eggs and yeast mixture. Stir until the dough comes together.
3. Remove dough from the bowl and place on a lightly floured surface. Knead for 5–8 minutes, until the dough becomes smooth and elastic.
4. Drizzle the bowl with oil, place the dough back in, and cover with plastic wrap or cloth.
5. Let rise until doubled, approximately 2 hours in a warm area. Or, if you plan to make these the next morning, place covered bowl into the fridge or store dough in a large sealed plastic bag and let sit in your refrigerator overnight. (If you let your dough rise overnight, remove from fridge and let come to room temperature before punching down, then continue to step 6.)
6. Once dough has doubled in size, punch down and dump onto a floured surface.
7. Roll into a circle approximately ½-inch thick.
8. Using a round dough cutter (2 ½ inches), cut out circles and cut out the dots in the center using a smaller round cutter.
9. Cover the dough rounds and let set for 30 minutes (on top of a warm oven).
10. Once the doughnuts have rested, start to heat your oil in a large pot or Dutch oven. The oil should be about 1 inch from the bottom of the pot and heated until 375 degrees. No higher otherwise it will brown the doughnuts too fast.
11. Once the oil is hot enough, plop in the doughnuts a few at a time. Do not overcrowd.
12. Fry until the bottoms are golden brown. Use a tong to flip the doughnuts to the other side, about 2 minutes per side.
13. Remove from oil and place on a tray lined with paper towels or a wire rack to remove excess oil.

For the glaze:

1. In a small bowl, combine heavy cream, powdered sugar, and vanilla extract. Whisk until a smooth glaze forms.
2. Dip the doughnuts in the glaze while still warm or dust in powdered sugar.
3. Top with sprinkles if desired.
4. Roll or dust the dots in powdered sugar.
5. Best served immediately. Store in an airtight container for up to 1 day.

Chapter 4

Cookies + Bars

Probably the most craved set of baked goods. There's nothing better than coming home to a fresh batch of homemade chocolate chip cookies or a pan of brownies. I wish I could say I did this more! I know how personal these bakes can be. Everyone has their favorite—it takes you back to being a kid, sneaking a bite of cookie dough or licking the spatula full of brownie batter before your sibling could get to it.

LIA'S TIP: Have cookie dough scooped and stored in the freezer in an airtight container. Bake off at your leisure, even if it's just one!

Chocolate Chip Cookies

Yield: 24 cookies

At the shop, we make jumbo chocolate chip cookies the size of your head. They've been dubbed "the best chocolate chip cookie" by many of our amazing customers! With perfect golden crispy edges, a soft gooey center, and a sprinkle of flaky salt for that sweet-and-salty balance, they're irresistible!

INGREDIENTS

1 cup unsalted butter, at room temperature

¾ cup granulated sugar

1 ¼ cups packed brown sugar

2 ½ cups all-purpose flour

1 teaspoon salt

½ teaspoon baking soda

2 eggs

1 Tablespoon pure vanilla extract

1 cup mini semisweet chocolate chips

1 cup semisweet chocolate chips

Flaky sea salt for topping

DIRECTIONS

1. In a mixer fitted with the paddle attachment, mix together butter and both sugars on medium speed until light and fluffy, 3–5 minutes.
2. In a separate bowl, whisk together the all-purpose flour, salt, and baking soda. Set aside.
3. In a small bowl, combine vanilla extract and eggs. Add into the butter mixture, one egg at a time, scraping well after each addition.
4. Gradually add the dry ingredients, mixing on low speed.
5. Fold in the chocolate chips.
6. Cover the bowl with plastic wrap and chill in fridge for at least 30 minutes prior to scooping.
7. Preheat oven to 325 degrees. Line a cookie sheet with parchment paper.
8. Using a medium cookie scoop, portion the dough into slightly mounded balls (68g) and place a few inches apart on the cookie sheet.
9. Using your palm, flatten the dough ball just a bit and top with a sprinkling of flaky salt.
10. Bake for 13–15 minutes, rotating halfway through, until golden and crisp around the edges. The centers should be lighter in color and slightly gooey.
11. Remove from oven, lightly tap the tray, and let set for 5 minutes prior to serving (if you can!).
12. Store in an airtight container for up to 3 days or freeze dough balls prior to baking for up to 1 month. Thaw prior to baking.

Oatmeal Sammie

Yield: 1 dozen sandwich cookies or 2 dozen regular cookies

This cookie is perfect on its own—buttery, crispy, chewy, and soft all at once. But sandwich it with browned butter buttercream, and it's on another level. Our take on the beloved oatmeal cream pie; you may think you'll only eat half, but moments later, you'll realize it's magically disappeared.

INGREDIENTS

Cookie dough:

2 cups all-purpose flour

1 Tablespoon cinnamon

1 ½ teaspoons salt

1 teaspoon baking soda

1 teaspoon baking powder

1 ½ cups unsalted butter, at room temperature

¾ cup granulated sugar

¾ cup + 1 Tablespoon packed brown sugar

2 eggs

2 ½ teaspoons pure vanilla extract

1 ½ cups raisins (feel free to omit)

2 ⅛ cups old-fashioned rolled oats

Browned butter buttercream:

1 ½ cups unsalted butter

2 cups powdered sugar

1 teaspoon pure vanilla extract

1 teaspoon heavy cream

Pinch of kosher salt

DIRECTIONS

1. In a medium bowl, whisk together flour, cinnamon, salt, baking soda, and baking powder. Set aside.
2. In a mixer fitted with the paddle attachment, mix together butter, sugar, and brown sugar on medium speed until light and fluffy, about 3–5 minutes. Scrape the sides of the bowl.
3. Crack eggs into a small bowl; add in vanilla extract. While mixing on low speed, add eggs into the butter mixture, one egg at a time, scraping the bowl after each addition.
4. Gradually add dry ingredients and mix on low. When flour is partially incorporated, stop the mixer and scrape down the bowl, then add the oats.
5. Mix on low until fully incorporated.
6. Add the raisins and continue to mix on low speed until just incorporated.
7. Leave dough in the bowl and cover with cling wrap or form dough into a round disc and tightly wrap in the plastic wrap. Chill in fridge for 30 minutes to an hour.
8. Preheat oven to 325 degrees.
9. Using a medium cookie scoop or spoon, portion the dough into 2 dozen balls, approximately 2 inches.
10. Line two sheet trays with parchment paper and line up cookies, leaving a few inches in between.
11. Using your palm, press down the cookies slightly and bake for 15–20 minutes, rotating halfway through, until the edges are golden brown.
12. Remove from the oven, lightly tap the tray, and let set for 5 minutes before moving the cookies onto a wire rack to cool.
13. For sammies, allow to cool completely while preparing the browned butter buttercream filling.

Brown butter buttercream:

1. In a small saucepan, melt the butter and cook until it smells nutty, toasty, and you see little brown specs. Swirl the pan every few minutes. (Do not burn!)
2. Let the butter cool and resolidify to room temperature. You can speed up this process by placing it in the fridge for 10 minutes.
3. In a mixer with paddle attachment, beat the butter on medium-high speed until light and fluffy, about 5 minutes.
4. Add in 1 cup of the powdered sugar, whip for 3–5 minutes, and scrape down the sides of the mixing bowl.
5. Add in the rest of the powdered sugar. Whip for another 3–5 minutes until the buttercream is super light and fluffy.
6. Add in vanilla extract and heavy cream. Mix on low for 1 minute.

Assembly:

1. Pair your oatmeal cookies side by side and bottoms up on a sheet tray.
2. Using a piping bag, pipe a circle of buttercream in the center of one of the cookie pairs, or you can easily plop some buttercream in the center using a cookie scoop or spoon.
3. Sandwich the other cookie on top of the cookie filled with buttercream to create a sammie.
4. Chill for approximately 30 minutes before serving so the buttercream does not squeeze out the sides when you dig in!
5. Store sammies in the fridge or the regular cookies at room temperature in an airtight container for up to 5 days. Freeze dough balls prior to baking for up to 1 month. Let thaw prior to baking.

Gingerdoodles

Yield: 2 dozen

A soft, chewy, delightful molassesy cookie. Gingersnap meets snickerdoodle—a match made in heaven. I love these, probably one of my favorite cookies—ever!

LIA'S TIP: Gently tap the tray when taking the cookies out of the oven to make the perfect crackle on top.

INGREDIENTS

1 cup unsalted butter, at room temperature

1 cup granulated sugar

1 cup packed brown sugar

2 eggs

2 teaspoons pure vanilla extract

½ cup molasses

4 cups all-purpose flour

1 teaspoon cinnamon

¼ teaspoon cloves

¼ teaspoon ground nutmeg

1 teaspoon ground ginger

1 ¼ teaspoons salt

2 teaspoons baking soda

White coating chocolate for dipping if desired

DIRECTIONS

1. Preheat the oven to 325 degrees. Line two baking sheets with parchment paper.
2. In a mixer fitted with the paddle attachment or by hand with a wooden spoon, mix together butter, sugar, and brown sugar until light and fluffy.
3. In a separate bowl, combine the dry ingredients: flour, spices, salt, and baking soda. Whisk together.
4. In a small bowl or cup, combine eggs, vanilla extract, and molasses. Add to the butter mixture, one egg at a time, and mix until combined. Scrape down the sides.
5. Gradually add the dry ingredients into the butter mixture. Mix until all ingredients are incorporated well.
6. Using a cookie scoop or spoon, portion the dough into 2 dozen cookies, approximately 2-inch sized balls. Arrange cookie dough onto prepared baking sheets, leaving a few inches between.
7. Prior to baking, roll into sugar or leave plain if planning to dip in white chocolate. Using your palm, flatten the tops slightly.
8. Bake 13–15 minutes, rotating the tray halfway, until cracks form across the entire cookie. Give the tray a little tap as you take it out of the oven.
9. Allow to cool completely.
10. If desired, melt white dipping chocolate and dunk part of the cookie in the chocolate. Set on a parchment-lined sheet tray to dry.
11. Store cookies in an airtight container for up to 4 days. Or store the dough balls in an airtight container or bag for up to 1 month. Let thaw before baking.

Biscotti

Yield: 2 dozen biscotti, 2 loaves

I'll never forget studying abroad in Italy, stuffing my already overpacked suitcase with bags of biscotti to bring home. For this recipe, I channeled my roots and, after much trial and error, crafted the perfect crisp biscotti for dunking into a cup of joe. I love how these let you get creative with add-ins and flavors—from classic almond to cranberry orange.

INGREDIENTS

1 cup granulated sugar

¼ cup unsalted butter, at room temperature

2 Tablespoons almond paste (optional)

1 teaspoon pure vanilla extract

2 eggs

½ teaspoon almond extract (optional)

2 cups all-purpose flour

1 teaspoon baking powder

½ teaspoon salt

Add-in options:

¾ cup mini chocolate chips, chopped pistachios, or sliced almonds

For cranberry orange add:

2 Tablespoons orange zest with the sugar at step 2

1 Tablespoon fresh orange juice at step 3

¾ cup chopped dried cranberries at step 5

To dip (optional):

1 cup white or dark coating chocolate

DIRECTIONS

1. Preheat oven to 350 degrees and line a baking sheet with parchment paper.
2. In a mixer fitted with the paddle attachment, add granulated sugar, butter, and almond paste. Mix together until light and fluffy.
3. Add in vanilla extract, then eggs one at a time, mixing well after each addition.
4. In a separate bowl, combine the flour, baking powder, and salt. Slowly add into the butter mixture until just combined.
5. Add in chocolate chips, almonds, or add-in of choice and mix until just combined.
6. Remove dough from the bowl using a bowl scraper or spatula and dump onto a lightly floured surface.
7. Divide the dough in half and roll into two equal loaves, approximately 10 inches by 2 ½ inches, and place on a baking sheet, leaving 3 inches of space in between since the dough will spread and poof up while baking.
8. Bake approximately 20 minutes, until loaves are lightly golden brown across the top, spring back when touched, and cracks form.
9. Remove from oven and let the loaves cool completely.
10. Lower oven temperature to 300 degrees.
11. Transfer the loaves to a cutting board and use a serrated knife to slice 1-inch diagonal slices.
12. Place a wire rack on top of the baking sheet or line a pan with parchment paper. Line up your biscotti side by side on the rack.
13. Bake for another 10–15 minutes, until the biscotti are lightly golden brown and dried all the way through.
14. Let cool, then dip into white or dark coating chocolate if desired.
15. Store in an airtight container for up to a week or freeze for up to 1 month.

St. Louie Cake

Yield: 1 9 x 13 pan

Our take on a St. Louis favorite, the "gooey butter cake." With a rich, buttery, cake-like texture, our St. Louie strikes the perfect balance of sweet and gooey—you'll be dying to dig in! Serve it up for breakfast or as a potluck treat.

LIA'S TIP: Add mini chocolate chips and swap white cake mix for chocolate cake mix to turn it into a delish chocolate chip St. Louie.

INGREDIENTS

Louie base:

½ cup unsalted butter, at room temperature

1 egg yolk

¼ cup all-purpose flour

1 ½ cups white cake mix

1 Tablespoon whole milk

½ teaspoon pure vanilla extract

Topping:

½ cup unsalted butter, at room temperature

½ cup cream cheese, at room temperature

½ cup granulated sugar

1 cup powdered sugar

1 cup cake flour

½ teaspoon salt

¼ cup corn syrup

2 Tablespoons whole milk

1 teaspoon pure vanilla extract

1 egg

¼–½ cup powdered sugar

DIRECTIONS

For the base:

1. Spray the bottom of a 9 x 13 baking dish/pan and line with parchment paper. Allow some of the parchment paper to hang off the edge for easy removal.
2. In a mixer fitted with the paddle attachment or using a hand mixer, combine the butter, yolk, flour, cake mix, milk, and vanilla and mix well until a thick but smooth batter forms
3. Using a spatula, spread the base evenly into the pan.

For the topping:

1. Preheat oven to 325 degrees.
2. In a mixer fitted with the paddle attachment or using a hand mixer, mix butter and cream cheese until well combined and smooth.
3. In a separate bowl, whisk together the dry ingredients: powdered sugar, granulated sugar, cake flour, and salt. Set aside.
4. In a measuring cup combine the wet ingredients: corn syrup, milk, vanilla extract, and egg. Set aside.
5. Add the dry ingredients into the butter mixture and mix until well combined. Scrape down the sides of the bowl.
6. Add in the wet ingredients and mix on low to combine.
7. Crank up the mixer speed to medium-high and mix until the batter is super light and fluffy. Scrape down the bowl a few times in between. It should be pale in color, fluffy and voluminous.
8. Pour the topping over the base. Using a spatula, spread the topping evenly across the base.
9. Bake for 20–25 minutes until the top is very lightly browned. The edges will be slightly darker than the center, and it will still be a little jiggly but will set as it cools.
10. Let cool and serve immediately, or wrap and store in the fridge for up to 3 days or in the freezer for up to 1 month.
11. Using a sifter, dust the top with powdered sugar prior to serving.

Fudgy Brownies

Yield: 1 9 x 13 pan

A riff on the classic "Cosmic Brownie," these are super, super fudgy. They remind me of devouring a Little Debbie brownie—one bite takes you right back. I love seeing a little kid at the bakery with chocolate all over their face and a big smile. Add a thin layer of silky ganache spread over the top—because, well, you deserve it.

INGREDIENTS

Brownie batter:

1 ¼ cups unsalted butter

2 cups semisweet chocolate chips

½ cup + 2 Tablespoons unsweetened cocoa powder

4 eggs

2 cups granulated sugar

4 ½ teaspoons pure vanilla extract

2 cups all-purpose flour

1 ½ teaspoons baking powder

¾ teaspoon salt

Ganache topping:

½ cup heavy cream

1 cup semisweet chocolate chips

½ teaspoon pure vanilla extract

Optional toppings or add-ins:

Powdered sugar for dusting (at step 10)

Ganache + jimmies for toppings (see page 53)

Fold in toasted pecans (at step 7)

Swirl in salted caramel (at step 8)

DIRECTIONS

For the batter:

1. Preheat oven to 350 degrees. Spray the bottom of a 9 x 13 dish/pan and line with parchment paper. Allow some parchment paper to hang off the edge for easy removal.
2. In a mixing bowl, whisk together flour, baking powder, and salt. Set aside.
3. In a microwave-safe bowl or using a double boiler, melt butter and chocolate chips together. Stir to combine.
4. Whisk in the cocoa powder until there are no lumps. It should be shiny, smooth, and melty. Set aside.
5. In a mixer fitted with the paddle attachment or whisking by hand, mix eggs, sugar, and vanilla extract until eggs become pale in color.
6. Slowly add in chocolate mixture. Mix well to combine.
7. Slowly add in the dry ingredients and mix until just combined. Scrape down the sides of the bowl, ensuring all ingredients are mixed well. Do not overmix.
8. Pour the batter into the pan. Using a spatula, spread out evenly.
9. Bake for 30–35 minutes, rotating the tray halfway through, until the edges begin to crack and the center is set.
10. Remove from the oven. Let cool prior to serving or adding the ganache.

For the ganache + topping:

1. In a small saucepan, heat the cream until tiny bubbles form around the sides of the pan. (Do not let come to a boil.)
2. Pour the cream over the chocolate chips and let sit for 2 minutes, or in a microwave-safe bowl, combine the cream and chocolate chips and microwave in 30-second intervals until the chocolate has melted.
3. Starting in the center, whisk the chocolate and heavy cream together until smooth.

Spread + serve:

1. Pour the ganache over the brownie and use a spatula to spread evenly across the top.
2. Sprinkle with jimmies. Let ganache set before cutting. Place in the fridge for a few minutes to help speed up this process.
3. Serve immediately or wrap and store in the fridge for up to 5 days or in the freezer for up to 1 month.

Chapter 5

Cakes + Cupcakes

Cakes are where it all began for me, so we're starting with the basics—simple recipes you can adapt, add flavors to, and turn into yearly traditions.

There are so many fun forms of cake. Get fancy with layers and fillings. Keep it simple with cupcakes or wow your guests with an elegant flourless cake. Whatever the celebration may be—go on and treat yourself and the ones around you.

LIA'S TIP: Baking cake layers or cupcakes a day or two ahead of time helps break up your time in the kitchen and ease the stress of baking, filling, and assembling all in one day. Once cooled, wrap tightly and freeze until it's time to assemble.

ALLERGY FRIENDLY: Any of my cakes can easily be made gluten-free; just sub all-purpose flour for gluten-free flour!

Classic Vanilla Cake

Yield: 8-inch 3-layer cake, or 2 dozen cupcakes

Everyone needs a classic vanilla cake recipe. It's been my tried and true for years. This isn't your typical box-mix cake that lacks in substance and flavor—it has body and richness. Best served at room temperature for ultimate texture and fluffiness.

INGREDIENTS

Cake batter:

1 ¼ cups whole milk, at room temperature

1 cup unsalted butter, softened

1 ½ cups + 2 Tablespoons granulated sugar

1½ cups all-purpose flour

1 ⅓ cups cake flour

1 Tablespoon baking powder

½ teaspoon salt

3 eggs + 1 egg white, at room temperature

1 Tablespoon pure vanilla extract

1 Tablespoon almond extract (optional)

Buttercream:

Vanilla buttercream (see page 59)

LIA'S TIP: Add almond extract for a traditional wedding cake flavor, lemon zest to brighten it up, sprinkles for fun, or layer it with homemade raspberry jam (see page 59)

DIRECTIONS

1. Preheat oven to 350 degrees.
2. Spray the bottoms of three 8-inch round cake pans with baking spray. Cut out a circle of parchment paper and place at the bottom of each pan.
3. Pour milk into a measuring cup and let come to room temperature.
4. In a mixer fitted with the paddle attachment or using a hand mixer, mix together the softened butter and sugar until light and fluffy for about 8–10 minutes, scraping down the sides of the bowl often.
5. In a separate bowl, sift together the dry ingredients: all-purpose flour, cake flour, baking powder, and salt.
6. In another separate bowl, combine eggs, egg white, and extracts.
7. Once your butter/sugar mixture is light and fluffy, add eggs one at a time until each is fully incorporated, scraping down the bowl after each addition.
8. Slowly add in ⅓ of the dry ingredients, mix well, and scrape down the bowl.
9. Next add in ½ of the milk, mix until combined, and scrape down the bowl.
10. Repeat this step by adding the dry ingredients, rest of the milk, and end with the rest of the dry ingredients.
11. Scrape the bowl well and make sure all ingredients are incorporated. The batter should look light, fluffy, and smooth.
12. Divide the batter evenly among the prepared cake pans.
13. Bake for 20–25 minutes, rotating the pans halfway through, until the cake is light golden brown and springs back when you touch it.
14. Let cakes cool completely, use a small spatula to run around the sides of the cakes to help loosen them, then pop them out of the pan and remove the parchment paper. Wrap tightly in plastic wrap and chill in the fridge if assembling same day. If preparing ahead of time, freeze overnight or up to 1 month.

Raspberry Layer Cake

Yield: 8-inch round cake, 3-layer cake

Show off with this beauty. Layers of simple vanilla cake and tart raspberry jam make it a showstopper in flavor and looks. Dress it up with fresh fruit and flowers, and give it a quick "naked" ice so the layers still shine through.

INGREDIENTS

Cake batter:

1 batch Classic Vanilla Cake (see page 56)

Raspberry jam filling:

1 12-ounce bag frozen raspberries (can use fresh)

1 Tablespoon lemon juice

¾ cup granulated sugar

1 Tablespoon cornstarch

Vanilla buttercream:

1 cup unsalted butter, at room temperature

3–3 ½ cups powdered sugar

4 teaspoons pure vanilla extract

2 teaspoons almond extract (optional)

2 Tablespoons heavy cream

Garnish:

Fresh raspberries or fruit of choice

Fresh flowers if desired

Tools needed:

Pastry bag

Icing spatula

Turntable (not 100% necessary but super helpful!)

DIRECTIONS

1. Prepare cake layers by following instructions for Simple Vanilla Cake (see page 56).
2. Prepare raspberry jam and vanilla buttercream (see below).

Raspberry jam:

1. In a saucepan, cook raspberries and lemon juice over medium heat until the raspberries have lost their shape, stirring occasionally.
2. Add sugar and let cook until sugar is dissolved, approximately 15 minutes. Continue stirring frequently to avoid burning the bottom.
3. Take a scoop of jam out and place in a small bowl. Whisk in the cornstarch to make a slurry and return it back into the saucepan.
4. Cook until the jam is thickened and bubby, about 5 minutes.
5. Let cool over an ice bath. Transfer to an airtight container and store in the fridge for up to 1 week or in the freezer for several months.

Vanilla buttercream:

1. In a mixer fitted with the paddle attachment, mix the butter until light and fluffy, about 10 minutes on medium-high speed. It should look pale in color, about two shades lighter than when started.
2. Slowly add in powdered sugar, ½ cup at a time, on low speed, then bring it to medium-high speed, mixing about 5 minutes after each addition of powdered sugar.
3. Once all of the powdered sugar is added and is at the sweetness level of your liking (add more powdered sugar if you like it sweeter), add in the vanilla and almond extracts and mix until light and fluffy.
4. Lastly, add in the heavy cream and mix for another 30 seconds.
5. If made ahead, store in the fridge in an airtight container. Place into a mixer and mix until light and fluffy before using.

Assembly:

1. Place one of the chilled cake layers on a serving plate or on a 10-inch round cake board and place onto a turntable.
2. Spoon buttercream into a pastry bag and make a pool or dam around the edge of the cake to help prevent the fillings from oozing out of the sides.
3. In the center of the dam, spoon half of the raspberry jam, approximately 6 ounces, into the center and spread evenly over the top of the first layer of cake.
4. Repeat steps for the next layer, finishing by placing the third cake layer on top.
5. Smooth the sides of the cake with a spatula, removing any excess filling or icing. Then place into the fridge to chill for at least 15 minutes before frosting.

6. Once the cake is chilled, use a spatula to spread the buttercream over the top and sides of the cake. Scrape away some of the buttercream on the sides to create a "naked" iced cake where you can see the layers of the cake shine through, or if you like more buttercream, spread it on evenly, creating a swoop-like texture.
7. Top with fresh florals and or fresh fruit if desired.
8. Serve immediately or store in an airtight container in the fridge for up to 3 days. Let cake come to room temperature before serving for best texture.

One Bowl Chocolate Cake

Yield: 8-inch, 3-layer cake

This one-bowl chocolate cake is one of the recipes I've had the longest. It's the first entry in my very first recipe book, covered in cocoa powder, grease, and frayed edges—well-used, well-loved, and shared with countless people. It's rich, moist, and will become your go-to chocolate cake recipe. Did I mention it's so simple to make? You literally need one bowl to whip it up!

INGREDIENTS

Cake batter:

2 ½ cups all-purpose flour

1 cup + 2 Tablespoons unsweetened cocoa powder

1 ¾ teaspoons baking powder

1 ¾ teaspoons baking soda

1 ¼ teaspoons salt

2 ½ cups granulated sugar

3 eggs

2 teaspoons pure vanilla extract

¼ cup + 2 Tablespoons sour cream

4 ½ Tablespoons canola or vegetable oil

¾ cup whole milk

1 cup + 2 Tablespoons warm coffee

Buttercream:

Chocolate buttercream (see page 65)

LIA'S TIP: The addition of coffee enhances the chocolatey flavor, but if you don't have any on hand, you can use warm water instead.

DIRECTIONS

1. Preheat oven to 350 degrees.
2. Spray the bottoms and sides of three 8-inch round cake pans with baking spray. Cut out three circles of parchment paper and place at the bottom of the pans.
3. Sift together dry ingredients: flour, cocoa, baking powder, baking soda, and salt into a mixing bowl.
4. In a mixer fitted with the paddle attachment or in a large mixing bowl with a whisk, combine the sifted dry ingredients plus the sugar, eggs, vanilla extract, sour cream, oil, and milk. Mix to combine.
5. Slowly drizzle in warm coffee while mixing on low speed. Mix until a smooth batter forms. It will be thin, but don't worry!
6. Divide batter evenly between the three pans.
7. Place into the oven and bake for approximately 20–25 minutes, or until the cake springs back when you touch the top. Rotate the pans halfway through.
8. Let cakes cool completely, then pop out of the pan and remove the parchment paper. Wrap tightly in plastic wrap and chill in the fridge. Freeze overnight or up to 1 month.

Chocolate Peanut Butter Cake

Yield: 8-inch, 3-layer cake

One of my winning challenges on *Next Great Baker,* my peanut butter chocolate cake was featured in *People Magazine*—so, you know, it's famous now. A household favorite since most people keep a jar of peanut butter in their cabinet. My nickname growing up was "Peanut Butter Cup," thanks to my uncle, Bob, and this cake brings me right back to snacking on my favorite childhood candy.

INGREDIENTS

Cake batter:

1 batch One Bowl Chocolate Cake (see page 62)

Ganache:

½ cup heavy cream

1 cup semisweet chocolate chips

½ teaspoon pure vanilla extract

Peanut butter fluff filling:

8 ounces cream cheese, softened

1 cup creamy peanut butter

½ cup powdered sugar

1 teaspoon pure vanilla extract

½ cup heavy cream

Chocolate buttercream:

1 ½ cups unsalted butter, at room temperature

2–2 ½ cups powdered sugar

1 ½ teaspoons pure vanilla extract

6 Tablespoons unsweetened cocoa

6 Tablespoons ganache

Pinch of salt

Tools needed:

Pastry bag

Icing spatula

Turntable (not 100% necessary but super helpful!)

DIRECTIONS

1. Prepare cake layers by following instructions for my One Bowl Chocolate Cake (see page 62).
2. Prepare ganache, peanut butter fluff, and chocolate buttercream (see below).

For the ganache:

1. In a small saucepan, heat ½ cup of heavy cream until tiny bubbles form around the sides of the pan. (Do not let come to a boil.)
2. Pour the heavy cream over the chocolate chips and let sit for 2 minutes, or you can go the microwave route. In a microwave-safe bowl, combine the cream and chocolate chips and microwave in 30-second intervals until the chocolate has melted.
3. Starting in the center, whisk the chocolate and heavy cream together until smooth. Stir in vanilla extract. Set aside to cool. You want it to be spreadable.

Peanut butter fluff:

1. Beat cream cheese and peanut butter in a mixer fitted with the paddle attachment until smooth and creamy. Add powdered sugar and vanilla extract. Beat until smooth.
2. In a separate or same bowl with a whisk attachment, whip ½ cup heavy cream, powdered sugar, and vanilla extract until firm stiff peaks form. Fold whipped cream mixture into the peanut butter mixture until light, fluffy, and combined.

Chocolate buttercream:

1. In a mixer fitted with the paddle attachment, mix the butter until light and fluffy, about 10 minutes on medium-high speed. It should look pale in color, about two shades lighter than when started.
2. Slowly add in powdered sugar, ½ cup at a time, on low speed, then bring it to medium-high speed, mixing about 5 minutes after each addition of powdered sugar.
3. Once all of the powdered sugar is added and is at the sweetness level of your liking (add more powdered sugar if you like it sweeter), add in the vanilla extract and mix until light and fluffy.
4. Sift in the cocoa powder. Mix to combine.
5. Add in 6 Tablespoons of ganache.
   Mix until fluffy.
6. If made ahead, store in fridge in an airtight container. Place into a mixer and mix until light and fluffy before using.

Assembly:

1. Place one of the chilled cake layers on a serving plate, or on a 10-inch round cake board on a turntable.
2. Spoon buttercream into a piping bag and make a pool or dam around the edge of the cake to help prevent the fillings from oozing out of the sides.
3. In the center of the dam, spoon 1 Tablespoon of prepared ganache into the center and

spread evenly over the top of the first layer of cake, then spread half of the peanut butter fluff over the ganache and top with the second cake layer.

4. Repeat steps for the next layer, finishing by placing the third cake layer on top.
5. Smooth the sides of the cake with a spatula, removing any excess filling or icing, then place into the fridge to chill for at least 15 minutes before frosting.
6. Once the cake is chilled, use a spatula to spread the chocolate buttercream over the top and sides of the cake, creating a swoop-like texture.
7. Serve immediately or chill for up to 3 days. Store any leftovers in an airtight container.

Kids' Favorite Chocolate Cherry Cake

Yield: 8-inch, 3-layer cake

My kids always get to pick their birthday cake theme and flavor, with endless options, but every year they choose the same: chocolate cherry! It's become a family tradition. Layers of moist chocolate cake and homemade cherry jam—in our house, we add a scoop of vanilla ice cream on top.

INGREDIENTS

Cake batter:

1 batch One Bowl Chocolate Cake (see page 62)

Cherry jam filling:

12 ounces fresh or frozen pitted red tart cherries (red tart are best but dark sweet can be used)

1 Tablespoon fresh lemon juice

½ cup granulated sugar

2 teaspoons cornstarch

Ganache:

½ cup heavy cream

1 cup semisweet chocolate chips

½ teaspoon pure vanilla extract

Vanilla buttercream:

1 cup unsalted butter, at room temperature

3–3 ½ cups powdered sugar

4 teaspoons pure vanilla extract

2 teaspoons almond extract (optional)

2 Tablespoons heavy cream

Tools needed:

Pastry bag

Icing spatula

Turntable (not 100% necessary but super helpful!)

DIRECTIONS

1. Prepare chocolate cake layers by following instructions for my One Bowl Chocolate Cake (see page 62).
2. Prepare cherry jam, ganache, and vanilla buttercream for assembly.

Cherry jam:

1. Place cherries and lemon juice into a saucepan and cook over medium-low heat until the cherries have lost their shape and are bubbly.
2. Add sugar to the pot and stir. Cook until sugar dissolves and bring to a boil.
3. Remove ¼ cup of liquid from your cherries into a small measuring cup. Stir in 2 teaspoons of cornstarch. Make sure there are no lumps. Add the slurry back into the cherries and continue to cook until the jam gets bubbly and thickens.
4. Pour the jam into a bowl and let cool over an ice bath or in the refrigerator.
5. The jam can be made in advance, stored in a mason jar or airtight container in the fridge for up to 5 days, or frozen for up to 1 month.

For the ganache:

1. In a small saucepan, heat the cream until tiny bubbles form around the sides of the pan. (Do not let come to a boil.)
2. Pour the cream over the chocolate chips and let sit for 2 minutes. Or, in a microwave-safe bowl, combine the cream and chocolate chips and microwave in 30-second intervals until the chocolate has melted.
3. Starting in the center, whisk the chocolate and heavy cream together until smooth.

Vanilla buttercream:

1. In a mixer fitted with the paddle attachment, mix the butter until light and fluffy, about 10 minutes on medium-high speed. It should look pale in color, about two shades lighter than when started.
2. Slowly add in powdered sugar, ½ cup at a time, on low speed, then bring it to medium-high speed, mixing about 5 minutes after each addition of powdered sugar.
3. Once all of the powdered sugar is added and is at the sweetness level of your liking (add more powdered sugar if you like it sweeter), add in the vanilla extract and almond extract and mix until light and fluffy.
4. Lastly, add in the heavy cream and mix until incorporated.
5. If made ahead, store in fridge in an airtight container. Place into a mixer and mix until light and fluffy before using.

Assembly:

1. Place one of the chocolate cake layers on a serving plate or on a 10-inch round cake board on a turntable.
2. Spoon buttercream into a piping bag and make a pool or dam around the edge of the

cake to help prevent the fillings from oozing out of the sides.

3. In the center of the dam, spoon in 1 Tablespoon of ganache and spread evenly over the top of the first layer of cake.
4. Spread half of the cherry jam over the ganache, about a ½ cup, and top with the second cake layer.
5. Repeat steps for the next layer, finishing by placing the third cake layer on top.
6. Smooth the sides of the cake with a spatula, removing any excess filling or icing. Then place into the fridge to chill for at least 15 minutes before frosting.
7. Once the cake is chilled, use a spatula to spread the vanilla extract buttercream over the top and sides of the cake. Smooth the sides with a spatula.
8. If desired, use a piping bag and star tip to pipe dollops around the top of the cake, and place a maraschino cherry on top of each dollop, or skip this step and just place the cherries around the top edge of the cake.
9. Serve immediately or store in an airtight container in the fridge for up to 5 days or freeze for up to 1 month.

Carrot Cake Slab

Yield: 9 x 13 cake pan/dish

I love a classic carrot cake—warm spices, flecks of freshly grated carrots throughout, and the addition of fresh carrot puree, a step that goes the extra mile to make it extra moist. Fold in nuts for crunch and shmeer the top with our cream cheese fluff for the perfect party dessert.

INGREDIENTS

Carrot cake:

1 cup carrot puree (3–4 medium carrots sliced + boiled)

½ cup granulated sugar

1 ½ cups packed brown sugar

2 teaspoons pure vanilla extract

1 ½ cups shredded carrots, approximately 2 large carrots

½ cup canola oil

4 eggs

¼ cup sour cream

2 ¾ cups all-purpose flour

2 teaspoons baking powder

2 teaspoons baking soda

1 teaspoon sea salt

1 Tablespoon cinnamon

¼ teaspoon nutmeg

⅛ teaspoon cloves

Cream cheese fluff:

10 ounces cream cheese, softened

¾ cup powdered sugar

¾ cup heavy cream

1 ½ teaspoons pure vanilla extract

DIRECTIONS

Carrot cake:

1. Prepare carrot puree by placing carrots in a saucepan with water to cover them. Bring to a boil and cook until carrots are tender and a fork can poke through.
2. Strain carrots and place them into a food processor or blender and puree until smooth. Set aside to cool.
3. Spray the bottom and then line a 9 x 13 cake pan/dish with parchment paper. Let the paper hang off the edge as this will help the cake lift out easier.
4. Preheat oven to 350 degrees.
5. In a mixing bowl, sift together dry ingredients: flour, baking powder, baking soda, salt, and spices.
6. In a separate mixing bowl fitted with the paddle attachment or by hand with a whisk, mix together sugar, brown sugar, vanilla extract, carrot puree, shredded carrots, and oil.
7. Add in eggs one at a time, mixing after each addition.
8. Add in the sour cream and mix until smooth.
9. Slowly add the dry ingredients into the wet ingredients. Mix well to combine until smooth.
10. Pour the batter into the pan. Using a spatula, spread the batter evenly across.
11. Bake for approximately 38–40 minutes until the top is golden and the cake springs back when touched.
12. Let cool completely while you prepare the cream cheese frosting.
13. Can be made ahead of time, wrapped tightly and frozen for up to a month. Let thaw before frosting.

Cream cheese fluff:

1. In a bowl fitted with the paddle attachment or using a hand mixer, mix the softened cream cheese until smooth, scraping down the bowl to ensure there are no lumps.
2. Add powdered sugar and mix to combine until smooth.
3. Scrape the cream cheese mixture into a separate bowl and set aside.
4. In the same mixing bowl, now fitted with a whisk attachment, add the cold heavy cream and vanilla extract. Whip until medium stiff peaks form.
5. Gently fold the whipped cream into the cream cheese mixture to create a super light and fluffy cream cheese fluff.
6. Store in an airtight container in the fridge for up to 1 week.

Assembly:

1. If desired, remove the cake from the cake pan by lifting the edges of the parchment paper and place onto a serving platter, or just leave the cake in the pan.
2. Using a spatula, spread the cream cheese fluff over the top of the carrot cake, creating a swoop-like texture.
3. Slice and serve right away or place into the fridge to chill if desired.
4. Place a lid over the cake or wrap with plastic wrap and refrigerate if you plan to serve it the next day.
5. Store leftovers in an airtight container in the fridge for up to 3 days.

Funfetti Cupcakes

(vegan)

Yield: 24 cupcakes

So many customers come in asking for a treat for their dairy- or egg-free child or friend. These cupcakes fill the void that so many kids with allergies face—they deserve something fun to celebrate with on birthdays or any day! It's a yummy cupcake everyone can enjoy.

INGREDIENTS

Cupcake batter:

1 flax "egg" (1 Tablespoon ground flax + 2 Tablespoons water)

1 cup vegan butter, room temperature

1 ½ cups + 2 Tablespoons granulated sugar

1 ½ cups all-purpose flour

1 ⅓ cups cake flour

½ teaspoon salt

½ teaspoon baking soda

1 Tablespoon baking powder

1 ¼ cups almond milk (or dairy-free milk of choice)

1 Tablespoon fresh lemon juice

1 Tablespoon pure vanilla extract

¼ cup rainbow jimmies

Vegan buttercream:

1 cup vegan butter, room temperature

1 cup shortening

2 cups powdered sugar

2 teaspoons pure vanilla extract

½ teaspoon fresh lemon juice

¼ cup rainbow jimmies for sprinkling

DIRECTIONS

For the batter:

1. Preheat oven to 350 degrees. Line two muffin trays with cupcake liners.
2. In a small bowl, make the flax "egg" by combining 1 Tablespoon of ground flax and 2 Tablespoons of water. Stir and let set for 5 minutes.
3. In a mixer fitted with the paddle attachment, mix together butter and sugar until light and fluffy.
4. Scrape down the sides of the bowl. There should be no yellow streaks.
5. In a separate bowl, sift together dry ingredients: flour, cake flour, salt, baking soda, and baking powder.
6. In a measuring cup, combine the wet ingredients: almond milk, lemon juice, and vanilla extract.
7. Add the flax egg into the butter mixture, and mix to combine, then add ⅓ of the dry ingredients to the mixture and mix on low to incorporate.
8. Scrape down the sides of the bowl, then add in half of the wet ingredients. Repeat with the remaining dry and wet ingredients, ending with the dry.
9. Fold in the sprinkles.
10. Fill the cupcake liners approximately ⅔ full.
11. Bake at 350 degrees for 13–15 minutes, until the cake bounces back when lightly touched and the tops are lightly golden.
12. While the cupcakes cool, prepare the vegan buttercream. The cupcakes can be baked ahead of time, wrapped tightly, and frozen prior to frosting.

For the buttercream:

1. In a mixer using the paddle attachment, mix vegan butter until light and fluffy, approximately 10 minutes, scraping down the sides often. There should be no lumps and the butter will look paler in color.
2. Add in shortening and half of the powdered sugar.
3. Mix on medium speed for 5 minutes. Scrape down the sides of the bowl several times.
4. Add the rest of the powdered sugar and mix for 5 minutes on medium-high until light and fluffy.
5. Add in the vanilla extract and lemon juice and mix to combine.

Assembly:

1. Using a cookie scoop or spoon, scoop a small mound of buttercream onto the cupcake.
2. Using a small offset spatula, go around the cupcake, bringing the frosting to the edge and creating a small mountain peak.
3. Then, using the spatula, make a divet or swoop in the center of the peak of buttercream.
4. Top with rainbow jimmies and serve immediately or store in an airtight container in the fridge for up to 3 days.

Flourless Chocolate Cake

(gluten-free)

Yield: 9-inch springform cake

If you're looking for a simple dessert to bring to a dinner party and impress your family or friends, this will be your new go-to! My baker Bri developed this decadent, rich, flourless chocolate cake. Top it with berries and a dusting of powdered sugar, and you'll give your guests something extra special to savor.

INGREDIENTS

1 ½ cups 72% dark chocolate, chopped

1 cup + 2 Tablespoons unsalted butter

1 ½ cups granulated sugar

½ teaspoon salt

7 eggs, room temperature

1 teaspoon pure vanilla extract

⅛ teaspoon almond extract (optional)

Garnish:

1 pint fresh raspberries

2 Tablespoons powdered sugar for dusting

DIRECTIONS

1. Preheat oven to 325 degrees. Spray with baking spray the bottom of a 9-inch springform pan and line with a circle of parchment paper.
2. Melt the chocolate and butter together in a heat-proof mixing bowl over a double boiler.
3. Remove from heat, and with a whisk stir the sugar into the chocolate mixture until well combined.
4. In a separate bowl, combine eggs and extracts. Add into the chocolate mixture, one at a time, stirring after each addition until the batter looks smooth and glossy.
5. Pour batter into the prepared pan and bake for approximately 40–45 minutes, rotating halfway through.
6. Remove from oven, let cool to room temperature, and then chill for at least 30 minutes before removing from the pan.
7. Remove cake from the springform pan and set on a serving dish.
8. Top with fresh raspberries and dust with powdered sugar prior to serving.

Mini Cheesecakes

Yield: 18 (1 ½ dozen)

Every summer, we get homegrown strawberries from the sweetest neighbor down the road, Leo, who's been growing them for decades. A dollop of whipped cream and Leo's insanely bright-red strawberries make these cheesecakes something you'll crave over and over again. The perfect size treat for those who want just a little sweet to end their meal.

INGREDIENTS

Graham cracker crust:

1 ½ cups graham cracker crumbs

⅓ cup granulated sugar

Pinch of salt

½ cup unsalted butter, melted

Cheesecake:

1 pound cream cheese, at room temperature

¾ cup granulated sugar

¼ cup sour cream

1 ½ teaspoons all-purpose flour

2 eggs

½ teaspoon pure vanilla extract

Whipped cream:

1 cup heavy whipping cream, cold

1 ½ Tablespoons powdered sugar

½ teaspoon pure vanilla extract

Topping:

Sliced strawberries or fresh fruit

DIRECTIONS

1. Preheat oven to 350 degrees.
2. Line the muffin pans with paper liners.

For the graham cracker crust:

1. Combine ingredients in a small mixing bowl, pour over the melted butter, and using a fork, combine until the texture of wet sand.
2. Add a scoop of graham cracker crust to the bottom of each liner and press down flat.
3. Par-bake the crusts for 5 minutes, remove from oven, and let cool.

For the batter:

1. In a mixer fitted with the paddle attachment or using a hand mixer, mix cream cheese until smooth with no lumps.
2. Scrape down the bowl several times to ensure the mixture is smooth.
3. Add in the sugar, mix.
4. Add in the sour cream and mix until well combined.
5. Add in the flour and mix on low.
6. Crack eggs into a small bowl; add in vanilla extract. Add eggs into the mixture, one at a time, until each is incorporated. Beat until mixture becomes light and fluffy.
7. Using a cookie scoop or spoon, divide cheesecake mixture evenly between the muffin tins.
8. Bake for approximately 15 minutes, rotating halfway through, until the tops have puffed up and spring back when touched. They will have a little jiggle but will set as they cool.
9. Remove from the oven and let cool to room temperature, then chill in the fridge for at least 30 minutes before serving, or freeze for up to 1 month and pull out to serve when desired.

Whipped cream:

1. In a mixer fitted with the whisk attachment or using a hand mixer, whip heavy cream, powdered sugar, and vanilla extract on high until medium peaks form.
2. Store in an airtight container in the fridge for up to 3 days.
3. Top each cheesecake with a dollop of fresh whipped cream and sliced strawberries, or fruit of choice.

Chapter 6

Pies, Galettes + Tarts

The most nostalgic of the bunch. There is something timeless and comforting about a homemade pie or tart. It's a dessert that tells a story. We'll start off with mastering my tried-and-true Master Pie Dough that is versatile enough for both sweet and savory bakes. Then we'll dive into an array of recipes that bring together bold flavors, textures, and a touch of nostalgia. Whether you're making a show-stopping Banana Brûlée Pie or a simple Rustic Fruit Galette, these recipes are designed to be made, shared, and remembered.

LIA'S TIP: Go the extra mile and make your crust from scratch. Every good pie starts with a solid foundation. Skip the store-bought filling too—your family and friends will appreciate this extra step, and I guarantee they will notice the difference!

Master Pie Dough

Yield: 1 9-inch pie crust, 1 large galette, 6 strudels, or 6 individual galettes

Mastering this pie dough will open doors to a world of endless recipes. You'll be able to create countless desserts with this simple, flaky, buttery dough—and my secret ingredient is a must! Pie dough can make or break a dessert, and trust me, it's worth it to make it homemade.

LIA'S TIP: Have a few pie shells stashed in your freezer, either before or after par-baking. This gives you the ease of pulling out a shell and whipping up a pie in a flash!

INGREDIENTS

½ cup unsalted butter, cubed + chilled

1 cup all-purpose flour

¾ teaspoon salt

¾ teaspoon baking powder

¼ cup sour cream (secret ingredient, shh!)

Pie weights or dried beans for par-baking

DIRECTIONS

1. Cut butter into 1-inch cubes and set aside.
2. In a mixer fitted with the paddle attachment or using a fork or pastry blender, combine flour, salt, baking powder, and cubed butter.
3. Mix on low speed until the butter has broken down to the size of peas.
4. Add in sour cream and mix until just combined. It's okay if it is a little crumbly; it will come together as it chills!
5. Dump dough onto a piece of cling wrap and wrap tightly.
6. Place in the fridge to chill at least 30 minutes or overnight before rolling. Can be frozen for up to 1 month.

Rolling + par-bake instructions:

1. Pull dough from the fridge, unwrap, and place onto a lightly floured surface.
2. Roll the dough out into a circle approximately ¼-inch thick and place into your pie pan.
3. Crimp the edges of the dough and chill again for at least 30 minutes.
4. Preheat the oven to 350 degrees.
5. Once chilled, place a piece of parchment paper over the pie crust. You want the parchment paper to be bigger than the pie, hanging off the edges.
6. Pour beans or pie weights on top of the parchment paper.
7. Bake the crust for 10 minutes.
8. Remove from the oven, and take off parchment and weights. Using a fork, dock (poke) the bottom of the crust a few times and bake for an additional 5 minutes until the bottom is lightly browned.
9. Set aside to cool before you add your pie filling, or wrap tightly and freeze for several months.

Rustic Fruit Galette

Yield: 1 large rustic galette

Galette is just a fancy word for a rustic, free-form pie. One of my favorite desserts to make because they're beautiful, super simple, and are fun to mix up the flavors using seasonal fruits. Simply roll out the dough, fill with fruit, fold the edges, and voilà! You've got yourself a lovely crowd-pleasing dessert.

INGREDIENTS

Pie dough:

1 batch Master Pie Dough (see page 86)

Frangipane:

6 Tablespoons unsalted butter, at room temperature

½ cup granulated sugar

¼ teaspoon salt

1 cup almond flour

2 Tablespoons all-purpose flour

1 egg

1 ½ teaspoons almond extract

Fruit filling:

6 medium-large peaches (skin on), apples (peeled first), or fruit of choice, sliced thin

2 Tablespoons lemon juice

3 Tablespoons granulated sugar

¼ teaspoon pure vanilla extract

Egg wash:

1 egg

1 ½ Tablespoon heavy cream

¼ cup raw sugar for sprinkling

DIRECTIONS

1. Make a single batch of pie dough from the Master Pie Dough (see page 86); do not par-bake this crust. Prepare the dough, wrap tightly, and let chill in the fridge prior to rolling.

Prepare frangipane:

1. In a mixer, combine butter and sugar; mix until light and fluffy.
2. Add in egg and almond extract; mix to combine.
3. Add in almond flour, flour, and salt; mix until fluffy.
4. Set aside.

Prepare fruit:

1. Thinly slice peaches or fruit of choice and toss with sugar, lemon juice, and vanilla extract in a mixing bowl. Let mingle so fruit has time to macerate.

Assembly:

1. Preheat oven to 400 degrees.
2. Remove dough from fridge and place onto a lightly floured surface. Begin to roll out the pie crust into a large circle about 14 inches round and ¼-inch thick.
3. Carefully transfer the dough onto a parchment-lined baking sheet.
4. Spread a layer of frangipane in a circle almost to the edge of the pie dough, leaving enough space to fold over the edges.
5. Place sliced peaches or fruit of choice onto dough; layer each slice into a circle creating a beautiful pattern, or just pile them on top.
6. Fold over excess dough using a bench scraper or hands, covering the outer edge of the fruit.
7. In a small bowl, whisk together 1 egg and 1 ½ Tablespoons of heavy cream. Using a pastry brush, brush the edges of the pie crust with the egg wash and sprinkle with raw sugar.
8. Place into oven and bake until crust is golden brown, for 35–40 minutes.
9. Let cool slightly, cut into slices, and serve! Add a scoop of vanilla ice cream if desired.
10. Best served immediately; store leftovers in the fridge for up to 3 days.

Banana Brûlée Pie

Yield: 1 9-inch pie

This recipe is adapted from one I saw on a PBS Create show. It was playing in the background, and I remember stopping in my tracks to voice-text the recipe into my phone: "1 banana, 1 egg, blend, brûlée." Later, when I checked my notes, I tried to decipher what Siri had translated. Though she didn't quite get my gibberish, whatever happened was pure magic. It tastes like an elevated banana cream pie—the elegant brûlée top adds the perfect crackle, making it feel sophisticated yet so simple to make.

INGREDIENTS

Pie dough:

1 batch Master Pie Dough (see page 86)

Banana filling:

2 medium ripe bananas, divided

¼ cup whole milk

1 can sweetened condensed milk (14oz)

2 eggs + 1 egg yolk

1 teaspoon pure vanilla extract

¼ teaspoon salt

⅛ teaspoon cinnamon

Egg wash:

1 egg

1 ½ Tablespoons heavy cream or whole milk

Brûlée topping:

3 Tablespoons granulated sugar

Blow torch

LIA'S TIP: Go get yourself a blowtorch! You'll thank me later when you smell brûléed sugar or toasted meringue for the first time.

DIRECTIONS

1. Make a single batch of pie dough and follow par-bake instructions from the Master Pie Dough (see page 86).
2. Preheat oven to 325 degrees.
3. In a blender, add whole milk, sweetened condensed milk, eggs and egg yolk, vanilla extract, salt, cinnamon, and one banana. Blend until smooth.
4. In a small bowl, whisk together one egg and 1 ½ Tablespoons of heavy cream. Using a pastry brush, brush the edges of the pie crust.
5. Slice the remaining banana and lay the slices at the bottom of the pie crust.
6. Pour the filling over the banana slices. (The bananas will float to the top!)
7. Bake at 325 degrees for 45–50 minutes on the middle rack. Move to the bottom rack and bake for 10 more minutes. The pie will still be slightly jiggly but set, and the top will be golden brown.
8. Let the pie cool at room temperature. Cover with plastic wrap and chill in the fridge for at least an hour before serving.
9. Prior to serving, sprinkle the top with a thin layer of granulated sugar. Using a blow torch, brûlée the top until toasty and caramelized.
10. Serve with a dollop of fresh whipped cream (see page 82) or vanilla bean ice cream if desired.
11. Store in the fridge for up to 2 days.

Not Your Grandma's Pumpkin Pie

Yield: 1 9-inch pie

A twist on a classic with my secret ingredient that adds a little *umph* to your traditional pumpkin pie. I look forward to it all year—it must be chilled with a big ol' scoop of fresh whipped cream on top. My mouth is watering just thinking about it. Make one, bring it to Thanksgiving, and I guarantee you'll be making it every year.

INGREDIENTS

1 batch Master Pie Dough (see page 86)

Pie filling:

8 ounces cream cheese, at room temperature

1 cup packed brown sugar

¼ teaspoon salt

2 teaspoons cinnamon

2 teaspoons pumpkin pie spice

⅛ teaspoon nutmeg

1 Tablespoon all-purpose flour

⅛ teaspoon cloves

15 ounces (1 can) pure pumpkin puree

½ cup unsalted butter, melted

2 teaspoons pure vanilla extract

3 eggs, at room temperature

Egg wash:

1 egg

1 ½ Tablespoon heavy cream or whole milk

DIRECTIONS

1. Make a single batch of pie dough and follow par-bake instructions from the Master Pie Dough (see page 86).
2. Preheat oven to 350 degrees.
3. In a mixer fitted with the paddle attachment, beat the cream cheese until light and smooth, scraping down the bowl often to ensure there are no lumps in the cream cheese.
4. In a small bowl, combine flour, brown sugar, salt, and spices. Stir to combine and set aside.
5. Add the pumpkin puree into the cream cheese; mix to combine.
6. Scrape down the sides of the bowl and mix in the melted butter and vanilla extract.
7. Add in the flour, brown sugar, and spice mixture and mix to combine.
8. Next, on low speed, add in the eggs one at a time, fully incorporating after each addition, but do not overmix after the last egg. Scrape down the sides of the bowl and give it one last stir.
9. In a small bowl, whisk together one egg and 1 ½ Tablespoons of heavy cream. Using a pastry brush, brush the edges of the pie crust. This will help give your crust a lovely golden color.
10. Pour the filling into the par-baked pie crust and bake for approximately 35–40 minutes until the edges of the filling start to brown and pull away from the sides of the crust and small cracks form around the edges. The center of the pie will have a little jiggle but will set as it cools.
11. Let cool completely, wrap, and chill in the refrigerator for at least 1 hour prior to serving, or it can be made ahead of time up to 3 days prior or frozen for up to 1 month.
12. Serve with a dollop of fresh whipped cream (see page 82).

Cherry Strudels

Yield: 6 strudels

A take on the classic cherry toaster strudel I ate as a kid—only you don't have to share the icing packets. (My brother always took two, leaving one of us kids without!) Our cherry strudels have been a top favorite at the shop, and I know they'll be a hit in your home.

INGREDIENTS

Pie dough:

1 batch Master Pie Dough (see page 86)

Cherry jam:

12 ounces fresh or frozen pitted red tart cherries

1 Tablespoon fresh lemon juice + zest from 1 lemon

½ cup granulated sugar

2 teaspoons cornstarch

Egg wash:

1 egg

1 ½ Tablespoons heavy cream or whole milk

Vanilla glaze:

½ cup powdered sugar

3 Tablespoons heavy cream

½ teaspoon pure vanilla extract

DIRECTIONS

1. Follow Master Pie Dough instructions (see page 86), form into a disc, wrap, and chill dough while preparing the cherry jam.
2. Place cherries, lemon zest, and lemon juice into a saucepan and cook over medium-low heat until the cherries have lost their shape and are bubbly.
3. Add sugar to the pot and stir. Cook until sugar dissolves and bring to a boil.
4. Remove ¼ cup of liquid from your cherries into a small measuring cup. Stir in 2 teaspoons of cornstarch. Make sure there are no lumps. Add the slurry back into the cherries and continue to cook until the jam gets bubbly and thickens.
5. Pour the jam into a bowl and let cool over an ice bath or in the refrigerator.
6. Can be prepared in advance, stored in a mason jar or airtight container in the fridge for up to 1 week or frozen for up to 1 month.

Assembly:

1. After the pie dough has chilled, place it on a lightly floured surface and roll into an 8 x 14-inch rectangle.
2. Cut dough in half lengthwise and then cut into 12 3 x 4-inch rectangles. Reroll the dough scraps to get additional rectangles if needed.
3. Place six of the rectangles in a row and the other six in a row below.
4. Whisk together the egg and heavy cream to make egg wash. With a pastry brush, egg wash the edges of six of the pie rectangles.
5. Take your prepared cherry jam and remove the majority of the extra cherry juice by placing it into a strainer. You want some goo but not too much, so it doesn't ooze out the sides.
6. Spoon 1–2 Tablespoons of cherry jam in the center of the dough, leaving space around the perimeter.
7. Take the other pieces of pie dough and place on top of the ones with cherries.
8. Using your fingers, press along the edges to seal the bottom with the top pieces. Using a fork, crimp around the edges.
9. Place the finished strudels on a parchment-lined baking sheet and brush the tops with egg wash.
10. Place tray into the freezer to chill for at least 30 minutes.

Bake + glaze:

1. Preheat the oven to 400 degrees.
2. Bake for approximately 15 minutes until the tops and bottoms are golden brown.
3. While your strudels are baking, prepare the vanilla glaze.
4. In a small bowl, whisk together the powdered sugar, heavy cream, and vanilla extract.
5. Using a small spatula or spoon, spread the glaze over the cherry strudels.
6. Enjoy right away or store in an airtight container for up to 3 days.

Garden Galettes

Yield: 6 5-inch round individual galettes

A burst of summer garden flavor. Fresh basil pesto and homemade ricotta with thinly sliced tomatoes and zucchini, a beautiful, flavor-packed, and delicate savory pastry!

LIA'S TIP: You can easily buy premade pesto and ricotta at the store, but I'm telling ya, it makes all the difference when you make it homemade! Prepare them ahead of time so you can assemble the galettes with ease.

INGREDIENTS

Pie dough:

1 batch Master Pie Dough (see page 86)

Mar Mar's ricotta:

½ cup heavy cream

1 ½ cups whole milk

¼ teaspoon sea salt

1 ½ Tablespoons fresh lemon juice

Pesto:

2 heaping cups fresh basil leaves

¼ cup pepitas, pine nuts, or walnuts

¼ cup parmesan cheese, if desired

¼ teaspoon salt

¼ teaspoon pepper

2 Tablespoons fresh lemon juice

1 Tablespoon water

½ cup extra virgin olive oil

Fresh veggies:

2 medium tomatoes, sliced

1 zucchini, thinly sliced

½ cup grated parmesan cheese for sprinkling

Egg wash:

1 egg

1 ½ Tablespoons heavy cream or whole milk

DIRECTIONS

1. Follow Master Pie Dough instructions (see page 86).
2. Once the pie dough has chilled, divide the dough into six dough balls, 54 grams each.
3. Roll each out on a lightly floured surface into 5-inch round circles and ⅛-inch thick.
4. Place onto a parchment-lined sheet tray and chill the rounds in the fridge for about 10 minutes before assembling.

Mar Mar's ricotta:

1. In a small saucepan, combine heavy cream, milk, and salt.
2. On medium-low heat, bring to a simmer. Small bubbles will begin to form around the edges. Stir occasionally.
3. Remove from heat and add lemon juice. Gently stir once. Let set for 5–10 minutes.
4. Place a sieve over a bowl and cover the sieve with a cheesecloth.
5. Pour the milk mixture through the cheesecloth and let sit for 15 minutes until the ricotta has thickened.
6. Transfer the ricotta into a small bowl. Use immediately or cover and store in the fridge for up to 5 days.

Pesto:

1. In a food processor, blend the basil, pepitas or nuts, parmesan cheese (if desired), salt, pepper, lemon juice, and water.
2. Pulse until the basil and nuts have broken down into small bits.
3. Slowly add in the extra virgin olive oil until the pesto develops a smooth yet textured consistency.
4. Store in an airtight container in the fridge for up to a week or freeze for several months.

Assembly:

1. Smear the center of the galette rounds with 2 Tablespoons of ricotta, then add 1 Tablespoon of pesto and smear it in with the ricotta.
2. Layer three slices of tomato and three slices of zucchini on top of the ricotta and pesto around the centers, leaving about an inch of dough around the edges.
3. Using a bench scraper, fold the outside edges of the dough around the vegetables.
4. In a small bowl, whisk together egg and heavy cream. Brush the edges of the crusts with egg wash and sprinkle with fresh grated parmesan cheese.
5. Chill for at least 30 minutes prior to baking.
6. Preheat the oven to 400 degrees.
7. Bake for 25–30 minutes until the bottoms and edges are golden brown.
8. Serve immediately. Drizzle with balsamic if desired or top with a fried egg to take it to another level.

Veggie Quiche

Yields: 1 9-inch quiche, 6–8 servings

The belle of the brunch. Endlessly versatile—have fun combining flavors with seasonal veggies, meat, cheeses, and herbs!

LIA'S TIP: Prep your pie dough, filling, and veggies the day before, so the next morning you can assemble and bake!

INGREDIENTS

1 batch Master Pie Dough (see page 86)

Filling:

8 eggs

½ cup whole milk

½ teaspoon sea salt

¼ teaspoon fresh cracked pepper

⅓ cup heavy cream

8–10 cherry tomatoes, sliced in half

¼ cup thinly sliced zucchini and/or yellow squash

½ Tablespoon fresh chopped parsley

½ Tablespoon fresh chopped chives

¼ cup shredded cheddar cheese

DIRECTIONS

1. Follow the Master Pie Dough recipe and par-baking instructions (see page 86).
2. Preheat oven to 350 degrees.
3. In a mixing bowl, whisk together eggs, heavy cream, milk, salt, and pepper.
4. Arrange sliced tomatoes, sliced zucchini, and chopped herbs in the bottom of the par-baked pie shell. Sprinkle in a layer of cheese.
5. Brush the edge of the crust with a little of the filling as your egg wash, and pour the filling over the veggies into the crust. The veggies will float to the top once baked.
6. Bake quiche for 45–50 minutes until the center has set and the top is lightly golden.
7. Remove from oven and let set for 5–10 minutes before slicing and serving.
8. Best served the same day. Tightly wrap with plastic wrap and store leftovers in the fridge for up to 2 days. If made the day ahead, remove from fridge, cover the top with foil, and place into a 300-degree oven and warm for 20–30 minutes, or until the center of the quiche is warm.

Rosemary

Lemon Meringue Tarts

Yield: 6 4 ¾-inch round removable tart pans or 1 9-inch tart

When I was a kid, my mom said she walked into the kitchen and found me making a lemon meringue pie. Back then, it was Jell-O Cook & Serve and a premade crust. I perfected that recipe over the years and brought it to New York City while filming *Next Great Baker*. I made hundreds of these lemon meringue tarts for the final challenge, which ultimately led to my win. They became a fan favorite when I was pastry chef at Hendel's, my sister and brother-in-law's restaurant, and now they're one of the most requested items at the shop. Looking back at that kid in my parents' kitchen whipping up a pie after school, she was determined. This recipe is near and dear to my heart, and now I'm passing it on to you.

INGREDIENTS

Tart dough:

½ cup unsalted butter, softened

1 cup all-purpose flour

½ cup powdered sugar

1 egg, beaten

½ teaspoon pure vanilla extract or ½ vanilla bean

Lemon curd:

6 eggs

½ cup + 1 Tablespoon granulated sugar

6 lemons zested + juiced (1 cup juice)

½ cup + 1 Tablespoon unsalted butter, cubed + softened

Meringue:

4 egg whites

¾ cup + 1 Tablespoon granulated sugar

2 Tablespoons corn syrup

3 Tablespoons water

DIRECTIONS

Tart dough:

1. In a bowl fitted with a paddle attachment, mix the butter until smooth.
2. In a separate bowl, sift together flour and powdered sugar, and then slowly add into the butter until mostly incorporated.
3. Whisk the egg with the vanilla extract and add into the mixer. Mix on low to combine. If dough is sticky, add a pinch more flour.
4. Place dough onto plastic wrap, shape into a flat circle, wrap, and refrigerate for at least 1 hour.
5. Remove from fridge, place dough onto a floured surface, and roll out to ¼-inch thick.
6. Cut out circles slightly bigger than the tart forms and press dough into forms, making sure the bottoms and sides are all even. Cut off excess dough from the top.
7. Dock (poke) the bottoms of the tarts with a fork, place onto a parchment-lined sheet tray, and chill or freeze until firm.
8. Preheat the oven to 350 degrees.
9. Bake the tart shells for around 20 minutes, until light golden brown.

Lemon curd:

1. Cut butter into cubes, set aside.
2. In a heat-proof mixing bowl, whisk together eggs, sugar, lemon zest, and juice.
3. Fill a saucepan with water, about ⅓ of the way up, and bring to a simmer.
4. Set the mixing bowl on top and whisk continuously over the heat.
5. Cook the curd to 170 degrees, or until it starts to thicken and you can see lines made from the whisk.
6. Take off heat and strain the curd into another bowl.
7. Slowly add in butter a few chunks at a time, whisking constantly until all of the butter is incorporated and melted.
8. Place plastic wrap over the top and press onto the curd to prevent a film from forming. Refrigerate for at least 1 hour before assembling the tarts.

Meringue:

1. Place the egg whites and a pinch of granulated sugar into a bowl of a stand mixer fitted with the whisk attachment.
2. In a small saucepan, add sugar, corn syrup, and water over medium-low heat.
3. Bring the mixture to 203 degrees and then start your mixer on low speed. Whip the whites until lightly frothy.
4. As your egg whites are whipping, continue to cook the sugar mixture until it reaches 248 degrees, then (very) slowly add the syrup into the whites in a steady stream, with the mixer on medium-low speed.
5. Once all the syrup is added, crank up to high speed and whip until stiff peaks form and the bowl is cool to the touch.

Assembly:

1. Remove the shells from the tart pans.
2. Using a cookie scoop or spoon, fill the tart shells with lemon curd, and smooth the tops for an even layer.
3. Place the meringue in a pastry bag with a large star tip and pipe a circle starting from the outside, working your way into the middle, or gently spread the meringue on top of the tarts with a spatula.
4. Toast the meringue with a pastry blowtorch, swirling around the top of the meringue. (One of my favorite smells in the world is toasted meringue!)
5. Serve immediately or store in an airtight container, and refrigerate up to 1 day. Can be frozen; thaw before serving.

Chapter 7

Breads + Rolls

There is something so satisfying about working with dough—the cool touch you feel when you knead it just right. Making bread brings me back to a simpler time, like the generations before me, when you can turn a few ingredients into something that makes you feel at home.

This chapter is full of honest recipes that will ultimately help you grow as a baker—from my versatile Everyday Loaf and cozy Brioche Cinny Rolls to the easiest Focaccia you will ever make. I want you to dive into these recipes. Make them often, not just once. With a little patience and the right techniques, you'll be able to master the craft of bread baking in no time!

Brioche Cinny Rolls

Yield: 1 dozen rolls

My longtime baker, Bri, developed this beloved "Bri Bri's brioche" recipe with a pop of orange zest in the glaze and a hint of flaky salt to offset the sweetness. Everything you would want in a cinny roll and more: tender, airy, and not overly sweet. One of my most memorable moments as a bakery owner was seeing people line up outside waiting for these babies. I guarantee your family will be impatiently waiting for them to come outta the oven!

LIA'S TIP: This is a 2-day process! Prep the dough and shape the day before so you can pull them out of the fridge in the morning to bake. The smell alone will be everyone's alarm clock.

INGREDIENTS

Dough:

¼ cup warm whole milk

3 ½ cups all-purpose flour

⅓ cup sugar

2 teaspoons salt

1 Tablespoon + ½ teaspoon Fleischmann's Active Dry Yeast

4 eggs, at room temperature

1 ¼ cups unsalted butter, at room temperature, cubed

Filling:

¼ cup granulated sugar

¼ cup brown sugar

1 teaspoon pure vanilla extract

¼ teaspoon salt

2 ½ Tablespoons cinnamon

½ cup unsalted butter, melted

Glaze:

2 cups powdered sugar

½ cup + 2 Tablespoons heavy cream

Zest from 1 orange

Flaky salt for sprinkling

DIRECTIONS

1. Combine water and milk into a measuring cup and warm to 105–110 degrees. Stir in yeast; set aside for 5 minutes.
2. In a mixing bowl fitted with the dough hook attachment, combine flour, sugar, and salt. Mix on low speed until incorporated.
3. Slowly pour in yeast mixture and add eggs one at a time, allowing each egg to incorporate after each addition.
4. Add in butter slowly, a few chunks at a time.
5. Let dough mix on medium-high speed until it pulls away from the sides of the bowl and forms a ball around the hook.
6. Once the dough ball forms, place into a bowl and cover with plastic wrap. Let rise about 1–1 ½ hours in a warm area until doubled in size.
7. Punch down the dough and place in the refrigerator for at least 1 hour to chill, or overnight.
8. Pull out dough and let sit at room temperature while you prepare the filling.

Filling + assembly:

1. In a mixing bowl, combine granulated sugar, brown sugar, vanilla extract, salt, cinnamon, and melted butter. Stir to combine.
2. Dump dough onto a floured surface and roll into a 12 x 24 rectangle.
3. Spread the filling in an even layer across the dough and roll into a log.
4. Cut into 12 2-inch pieces and place in a parchment-lined 9 x 13 pan.
5. Cover and let rise for 1 hour, then place in the fridge to proof overnight.

Bake + glaze:

1. The next morning pull cinnamon rolls out of the fridge and let sit at room temperature for 30 minutes to 1 hour.
2. Preheat oven to 375 degrees. Bake cinnamon rolls for 30–35 minutes, rotating halfway through, until the tops are lightly golden brown.
3. While the cinny rolls are baking, prepare your glaze. In a small bowl, combine powdered sugar, heavy cream, vanilla extract, and orange zest. Stir until smooth; set aside.
4. Remove from oven, sprinkle the tops with a little flaky salt, and shmeer the glaze all over the tops of the cinny rolls.

Everyday Loaf

Yield: 1 free-form loaf

I remember when I was writing down my chicken scratch recipe and Max said, "What are you making?" And I was like, "Oh, just throwing a little of this and that in a bowl and calling it bread." And that's how the Everyday Loaf was born, a simple experiment turned into a household favorite that we've made time and time again. So versatile, so simple. Great for dipping, for toast, and for sandwiches. The flavor add-ins are endless. You'll want to make this for everyday living. I love to fill up a small plate with extra virgin olive oil, a drizzle of balsamic, and fresh grated parmesan cheese, and just dive right in.

INGREDIENTS

Classic loaf:

¾ cup warm water + 2 Tablespoons water, divided

1 ¾ teaspoons Fleischmann's Active Dry Yeast

2 cups + 2 Tablespoons all-purpose flour + extra for kneading

½ teaspoon granulated sugar

¾ teaspoon salt

1 Tablespoon extra virgin olive oil + more for coating the bowl

1 teaspoon honey

Flaky salt for sprinkling

LIA'S TIP: Jazz it up with my flavor variations on page 115!

DIRECTIONS

1. In a measuring cup, add ¾ cup warm water (105–110 degrees, the water should be warm but not hot) and the yeast. Stir to combine and set aside for at least 5 minutes.
2. In a large mixing bowl, combine flour, sugar, salt, 1 Tablespoon olive oil, and honey.
3. Pour the water and yeast mixture over the dry ingredients.
4. Using a spatula or wooden spoon, mix together until a shaggy dough forms. Add in the additional 2 Tablespoons of water, if needed, and mix until all ingredients come together and the dough forms an imperfect ball. (I like to get my hands dirty and mix by hand!)
5. Dump the dough out of the bowl and onto a lightly floured surface.
6. Knead the dough back and forth with your hands until a smooth and elastic dough forms and the dough begins to feel cool to the touch, 5–7 minutes.
7. Add a little olive oil into the same large mixing bowl, lightly coating the bottom and sides of the bowl.
8. Place the dough back into the bowl and cover with cling wrap or a damp cloth. Let dough rest (proof) for 1 hour in a warm area or on top of the oven.

Shape + bake:

1. After the dough has rested, remove from the bowl and place onto a lightly floured surface. Press/flatten the dough into a rectangle approximately 5 x 8 inches.
2. Fold the dough into thirds like a letter. Grab the bottom of the dough and fold it into the center, then bring the top of the dough over that.
3. Then fold the dough in half longways and pinch the seam together all the way across. Roll over so the pinch seam is facing down.
4. Gently place onto a parchment-lined sheet tray, creating an oblong loaf, tightly tucking in the sides around the bottom before it takes a little rest.
5. Add a light brush of olive oil on top, cover with cling wrap or a damp cloth, and let rise/proof for another 30–45 minutes, until doubled in size.
6. Preheat the oven to 475 degrees.
7. Once the dough looks doubled in size and bouncy, score the top of the dough with 3 diagonal slashes. Brush or pat the top with water and sprinkle with flaky salt.
8. Place into the oven on the middle rack, making sure there is enough room above to puff up.
9. Bake for 15–18 minutes until there is a nice golden color on the top and bottom and it sounds hollow when you tap it.
10. Let cool before slicing for at least 10–15 minutes for proper texture to develop.
11. Store in an airtight bag, wrap in foil for several days, or freeze for up to a month.

CRANBERRY ORANGE

Ingredients:

½ cup dried cranberries, roughly chopped

½ heaping Tablespoon orange zest

½ Tablespoon fresh-squeezed orange juice

Directions:

1. Add ingredients into flour mixture at step 2.

ROSEMARY + OLIVE

Ingredients:

¼ cup chopped pitted Castelvetrano olives

1 Tablespoon fresh chopped rosemary

Directions:

1. Add ingredients into flour mixture at step 2.

HONEY + OAT

Ingredients:

¼ cup rolled oats + ¼ cup for topping

2 Tablespoons honey (leave out granulated sugar)

Directions:

1. Add ¼ cup oats and honey into flour mixture at step 2.
2. Follow recipe as directed.
3. At step 5 in "shape and bake," gently pat or brush the top of the of the dough with water. Sprinkle a layer of oats on the top of the dough and proceed to baking.

CINNY RAISIN

Ingredients:

½ cup raisins

1 ½ Tablespoons unsalted butter, melted

¼ cup granulated sugar

1 teaspoon cinnamon

Directions:

1. Add raisins in with the flour ingredients at step 2.
2. In a separate small bowl, combine melted butter, sugar, and cinnamon.
3. Once you have reached “shape and bake” step 1, flatten into a rectangle and spread the cinnamon sugar mixture evenly over the dough, then proceed to step 2.

Pita + Hummus

Yield: 12 pitas

Some nights for dinner we have snack boards, a favorite in our house. Pita + Hummus is always the star. Homemade pita, hummus, and a bunch of fresh veggies to dip in. The perfect addition to your charcuterie board.

LIA'S TIP: Prep hummus ahead of time. We love having it on hand in our fridge for a quick snack or addition to our dinner. The pita can also be made ahead and frozen. Pop them out of the freezer and warm in the oven prior to serving.

INGREDIENTS

Pita dough:

2 ¼ teaspoons Fleischmann's Active Dry Yeast (1 packet)

2 cups warm water

5 cups all-purpose flour

1 Tablespoon granulated sugar

2 teaspoons salt

Extra virgin olive oil for coating the bowl + brushing

Hummus:

1 can chickpeas, drained + rinsed

1 Tablespoon tahini

1 Tablespoon lemon juice

¼ teaspoon paprika

Pinch of salt

2–4 Tablespoons ice water

3 Tablespoons extra virgin olive oil

1 Tablespoon fresh dill + parsley, chopped

DIRECTIONS

Pita:

1. In a small bowl, combine yeast, warm water (105–110 degrees), and sugar. Let sit for 5 minutes.
2. In a large bowl, combine flour and salt. Stir and make a well in the center.
3. Pour the yeast mixture into the flour and mix by hand or with a wooden spoon until a shaggy dough forms.
4. Cover and let rest for 20 minutes.
5. Remove the dough from the bowl and dump onto a lightly floured surface.
6. Knead the dough for 10 minutes, until a smooth and elastic dough forms.
7. Lightly coat the large bowl with olive oil and place the dough into the bowl.
8. Cover with plastic wrap or a cloth and let rise in a warm area (on top of the oven) for 1 hour.
9. While the dough is rising, prepare the hummus.
10. Once the dough has doubled in size, punch it down and divide into 12 balls, approximately 100 grams each.
11. Roll into buns and place onto a parchment-lined baking sheet or onto a clean surface. Cover and let rest for 20 minutes.
12. Preheat oven to 500 degrees.
13. On a lightly floured surface, roll each dough round into a thin circle.
14. Place on a parchment-lined baking sheet, leaving space between, and lightly brush the tops with extra virgin olive oil.
15. Bake until the pitas puff up and are lightly golden on top, about 8–10 minutes.

Hummus:

1. Drain and rinse the chickpeas and place into a food processor.
2. Add tahini, lemon juice, paprika, and salt and blend on high.
3. Add in ice water 1 Tablespoon at a time until you reach the consistency of your liking. Blend on high for 2–3 minutes until smooth.
4. Scrape down the sides and slowly drizzle in the olive oil while it is blending. Blend until smooth.
5. Store in an airtight container in the fridge for up to 5 days.
6. To serve, spread hummus into a flat bowl or dish. Drizzle a generous pour of extra virgin olive oil around the perimeter of the hummus. Top with fresh chopped parsley, dill, and a sprinkling of paprika.

Grandpa Petti's Knots

Yield: 2 dozen rolls/knots

My great-grandpa Petti had a passion for bread baking. The memory of his tender dinner rolls served at our family gatherings will always be cherished. I took his traditional recipe, adapted it slightly, and turned it into knots. I like to make this dough just as he did, with his hands. This recipe has been a part of my family for generations and will continue to be passed down for many more.

INGREDIENTS

2 ½ Tablespoons Fleischmann's Active Dry Yeast

¼ cup + 1 teaspoon granulated sugar, divided

3 cups warm water, divided

8 ¼ cups + 2 Tablespoons all-purpose flour

¼ cup extra virgin olive oil or vegetable oil

3 teaspoons salt

1 egg

For topping before baking:

Sesame seeds, flaky salt, and/or poppy seeds

Egg wash:

1 egg

2 Tablespoons water

LIA'S TIP: This recipe works great for dinner rolls, knots, or a classic Italian loaf.

DIRECTIONS

1. In a small bowl, mix yeast, 1 teaspoon sugar, and 1 ½ cups warm water (105–110 degrees). Let set until foamy, about 5 minutes.
2. In a large bowl, combine the flour, remaining 1 ½ cups water, oil, salt, sugar, egg, and yeast mixture.
3. Mix with a wooden spoon until ingredients start to come together; mix until dough forms.
4. On a floured surface, knead the dough until smooth, about 10 minutes.
5. Lightly coat a large clean bowl with olive oil. Place the dough in the bowl and lightly oil the top. Cover with plastic wrap or a towel. Let rise for 1 hour in a warm area. (You can proof the dough overnight in the fridge, remove the next day, and continue to the next step.)
6. Once the dough has doubled in size, punch it down.
7. Divide the dough into 24 pieces, roughly 65–70 grams per piece.
8. Using your hands, gently roll the piece of dough into a long log shape and tie into a knot.
9. Place the knots on a parchment-lined baking sheet, leaving space between. Cover with plastic wrap or cloth and let rise for 1 hour until doubled in size.
10. While the knots are resting, preheat the oven to 350 degrees.
11. Once the knots have finished their rise, brush the tops with egg wash and sprinkle with flaky salt, sesame seeds, or poppy seeds if desired.
12. Bake for approximately 25–30 minutes until golden brown on top.
13. Serve immediatley, or store in an airtight bag or container for up to 2 days. Store extras in freezer for up to 1 month; pull out to thaw and warm in the oven prior to serving.

Master Focaccia

Yield: 1 half sheet pan

The easiest bread you'll ever make. No knead, no time, no mess, no fuss.

Learning one base dough will give you the chance to be creative in the kitchen. My Master Focaccia is simple, one you can make the day before and proof overnight in the fridge or have it ready in a few hours for same-day baking. It's light and airy with the perfect amount of chew.

LIA'S TIP: Keep it classic and bake on a sheet pan, turn into focaccia babies, or use as a base for Friday night pizza. You'll be making this dough in various forms, time and time again!

INGREDIENTS

1 ¾ cup warm water

2 ¼ teaspoons Fleischmann's Active Dry Yeast

3–3 ½ cups all-purpose flour

2 teaspoons kosher salt

For topping:

¼–½ cup extra virgin olive oil for coating/drizzling

1 teaspoon flaky salt for sprinkling

1 Tablespoon fresh or dried herbs for topping if desired

DIRECTIONS

1. In a large bowl, mix water, yeast, flour, and salt together until a shaggy dough forms. It will look a bit messy, but that's okay!
2. Lift the dough out and lightly coat the bowl with olive oil. Place the dough back into the bowl, turn over to coat in the olive oil, and cover with plastic wrap or cloth. Let rise for 30 minutes on top of the oven or in a warm area until doubled in size.
3. Instead of kneading on a counter, you will perform a series of folds in the mixing bowl. After the 30 minutes are up and the dough has doubled, make your first fold by grabbing the edge of the dough, stretching it up, and folding it back over the rest of the dough. Repeat this 2–3 times so that all the dough gets evenly incorporated.
4. Cover with plastic wrap and let rise for another 30 minutes.
5. Repeat the folding process again. Cover and rest for another 30 minutes.
6. After the 30 minutes are up, the dough should look jiggly and bubbly.
7. At this step you can deflate the dough by punching it down. Cover the bowl with plastic wrap and place it into the fridge overnight to rest. When you are ready to bake next day, see step 9.
8. For same-day baking, continue to step 10.
9. For next-day baking, pull the dough out of the fridge and continue to step 10.
10. Line a sheet tray with parchment paper, drizzle with a generous amount of extra virgin olive oil, and dump the dough onto the tray. Let rest for at least 15 minutes.
11. Preheat the oven to 475 degrees.
12. Gently stretch out the dough almost to the edges of the sheet tray while poking holes into it with your fingers. It is important to be gentle with the dough and not press out all of the bubbles. If the dough resists, don't force it. Let it rest for a few minutes before continuing to stretch.
13. Once the dough has stretched close to the edges of the pan, drizzle the top with extra virgin olive oil and top with flaky salt, fresh herbs, or toppings of choice.
14. Place into the oven and bake for 15 minutes or until the top and bottom are golden brown.
15. Let cool slightly before slicing and serving.
16. Serve immediately. Store extras in an airtight bag or container for several days. Warm or pop in the toaster prior to serving.

Focaccia Babies

Yield: 1 half sheet pan

Instead of using sourdough like we do at the shop, I wanted to simplify our recipe for you by using my Master Focaccia dough to create these delicious focaccia babies. Jazz them up with toppings like lemon + thyme, rosemary + sliced olives, or tomato jam + basil prior to baking.

INGREDIENTS

1 batch Master Focaccia dough (see page 120)

Topping:

1 Tablespoon fresh chopped rosemary

1–2 teaspoons flaky salt for sprinkling

Extra virgin olive oil for drizzling

Alternative topping ideas:

Lemon zest + dried thyme

Sliced green olives + fresh rosemary

Sliced cherry tomatoes + fresh basil

LIA'S TIP: Individual servings are great for a dinner party, or slice them in half for sandwiches or veggie burgers.

DIRECTIONS

1. Follow directions for Master Focaccia dough (see page 120) through step 11.
2. Once you have followed the steps and your dough is on the sheet tray, use your fingers to gently press the dough into a rectangle, approximately 8 ½ x 11 inches.
3. Using a bench scraper, cut the dough in half longways, then cut into eight rectangles approximately 3 x 4 inches. Gently separate each rectangle, leaving a little space between, but it's also okay if they are close together.
4. Sprinkle the tops with flaky salt and fresh rosemary or toppings of choice.
5. Bake at 475 degrees for approximately 20–22 minutes until the tops and bottoms are golden brown.
6. Serve immedietly or store in an airtight container or bag for up to 2 days or in the freezer for up to 1 month. Warm in the oven prior to serving.

Sheet Pan Pizza

Yield: 1 sheet pan pizza

We have Friday pizza night in our house every week. Now let's be real; most of the time we order from our fav pizza shop, but when we make our crust from scratch, I go for ease: a simple Sicilian-style sheet pan pizza using my Master Focaccia (see page 120). It's the perfect base for your favorite pizza toppings, a crowd pleaser and a fun way to get the whole family involved in the kitchen.

LIA'S TIP: Par-bake the crust for a more even bake and a crisp crust all the way through. It can be made earlier in the day, so all you have to do is top and bake at dinner time.

INGREDIENTS

Pizza dough:

1 batch Master Focaccia dough (see page 120)

Pasta sauce:

14-ounce can San Marzano whole peeled tomatoes

Sea salt + fresh cracked pepper + seasonings of choice, to taste

½ Tablespoon chopped fresh basil

Pinch of granulated sugar

Pizza toppings:

12 ounces grated/shredded cheese of choice

Ideas:

Roasted zucchini + bell peppers

Sautéed mushrooms + black olives

Pepperoni + crumbled bacon

DIRECTIONS

1. Follow the directions from the Master Focaccia dough (see page 120) through step 10.
2. Dump the dough onto a parchment-lined baking sheet generously coated with extra virgin olive oil. Gently dimple and stretch dough to the edges of the sheet tray. If the dough starts to resist, stop stretching and let it rest a few minutes before you continue.
3. Once the dough has reached the edges, lightly cover with plastic wrap and let rest for 5–10 minutes.
4. Preheat oven to 500 degrees.
5. Gently dimple the dough again, focusing on the center areas, leaving a small perimeter without.
6. Par-bake the crust for 12–14 minutes on the middle rack until light golden brown throughout.
7. Remove from the oven and let it rest while you prepare the sauce and toppings.

Simple pizza sauce:

1. Place the San Marzano tomatoes into a small bowl. Using your hands (my kids love this step), mash up the tomatoes. It's okay if there are some smaller chunks!
2. Pour the tomatoes into a small saucepan. Add salt, pepper, and fresh basil. Bring to a simmer and cook for 15 minutes. Set aside.
3. Prepare your toppings of choice: sautéed veggies, sliced olives, pepperoni, etc. If using veggies, be sure to sautée or roast prior in order to eliminate any excess liquids.

Top + bake:

1. Lower oven to 475 degrees.
2. Shmeer a layer of pizza sauce on top of the focaccia, leaving it a little bare around the edges for crust if desired.
3. Next add a thin sprinkle of cheese (not all of your cheese yet!) and layer on the toppings. Place into the oven on the middle rack and bake for 10–12 minutes.
4. Pull out of the oven and add another layer of cheese, then move it to the top rack and bake for an additional 5 minutes until the cheese is melty, bubbly, and lightly browned.
5. Remove from the oven and let rest for 10 minutes before slicing and serving.
6. Serve immediately. Store leftovers in an airtight bag or container in the fridge for up to 2 days. Warm prior to serving.

Index

Made
CRAFT BAKE
CAKES
COFFEE

y Lia
SWEETS
SWAG

Way to Cook
Julia Child